THE WINNIPEG GENERAL STRIKE

SOCIAL CREDIT IN ALBERTA

ITS BACKGROUND AND DEVELOPMENT

A series of studies sponsored by the Canadian Social Science
Research Council, directed and edited by S. D. Clark.

1. *The Progressive Party in Canada.*   *By* W. L. MORTON
2. *The Winnipeg General Strike.*   *By* D. C. MASTERS

⇛ THE ⇚
Winnipeg General Strike

By
⇛ D. C. MASTERS ⇚

Professor of History
Bishop's University

UNIVERSITY OF TORONTO PRESS
Toronto, 1950

Copyright, Canada, 1950
by University of Toronto Press

Printed in Canada

London: Geoffrey Cumberlege
Oxford University Press

SCHOLARLY REPRINT SERIES
ISBN 0-8020-7018-3
LC 51-5058

Donald C. Masters

TO THE MEMORY OF
A. A. MacDONELL

Foreword

T H I S is the second of a series, sponsored by the Canadian
Social Science Research Council, through a special grant from
the Rockefeller Foundation, relating to the background and
development of the Social Credit movement in Alberta. The first
of the series, *The Progressive Party in Canada* by W. L. Morton,
was concerned primarily with the agrarian revolt in western
Canada in the years immediately after the first world war.
Professor Masters' study is concerned with the closely parallel
movement of labour revolt. Organization of the One Big Union
in western Canada coincided almost exactly in time with the
organization of the Progressive party. Labour tested its economic strength in the Winnipeg general strike in 1919 and its
political strength in the federal election of 1921. The farmers,
postponing economic action until 1924 when the wheat pools
were launched, threw their whole political weight into the
federal and provincial election battles of 1921 and 1922 and
captured the governments of Alberta and Manitoba. Spread
of the Progressive movement into central and eastern Canada
was paralleled by the spread eastward of industrial unionism
and the outbreak of a general strike in Toronto, but both the
agrarian and the labour movement were essentially western in
their philosophy and appeal.

Although these movements developed in sharp antagonism
to one another, they nevertheless had much in common. Both
the One Big Union and the Progressive party were expressions
of protest against eastern dominance. This dominance mani-
fested itself not only through the organized financial and
business interests of central Canada but also through those
economic and political and cultural organizations, such as trade
unionism, the federal parties, and the churches, which claimed
to serve western as well as eastern interests. The One Big
Union was organized in direct challenge to the leadership of
the Trades and Labor Congress much as the Progressive party
grew up in challenge to the leadership of the Liberal party.

Central Canadian labour, which had developed a militant tradition in the organization of the Knights of Labor, had after 1900 become gradually more and more conservative with the growing influence of the powerful craft unions in the Trades and Labor Congress. Rapid wartime expansion of the manufacturing and construction industries and of transportation services, together with increasing economic prosperity, strengthened greatly the bargaining position of these old established unions and provided them with important vested interests to protect. Western labour, in a frontier economy dependent upon uncertain markets, found itself with no effective organization to champion its interests, and failure to break the hold of the eastern unions on the Trades and Labor Congress led to the break of 1919 and to the movement to organize the One Big Union.

The close American connection of the western Canadian labour movement emphasized the break with eastern labour. The One Big Union in western Canada, like the Industrial Workers of the World in the western United States, was a product of the frontier. The isolation of the industrial and mining communities of the West made necessary the joining of labour in one closely integrated organization. Industrial unionism, by bringing about the combination of labour within the whole industry, and to a degree within the whole local community, implied the separation of the industrial West from the older industrialized East. The O.B.U. developed in the tradition of American frontier radicalism. It was a separatist movement of much the same sort as the Progressive movement. The object was to place control in the hands of locally organized labour and thus destroy the power of outside industrial interests. In this sense the movement was revolutionary. Achievement of the ends of industrial unionism would have meant the almost complete economic autonomy of the western industrial communities. With such economic autonomy attained through organized labour, political control from the outside could have had little meaning.

Yet the western Canadian labour movement was not a simple projection of the western American labour movement. As Professor Masters has shown, the leaders of the O.B.U. and the members of the Winnipeg strike committee were mostly

men who had secured their early training in trade unionism in
Great Britain. However radical these men may have been,
their radicalism was not in the tradition of the American
frontier. In an American setting, they were almost bound to
exert a moderating influence; they were Britishers living abroad
in one of the colonies and their Britishism came into conflict
with the hard, politically irresponsible radicalism of the American frontier. In the western labour movement the British
industrial unionist played a role somewhat like that which the
British Wesleyan had played, much earlier, in the Canadian
Methodist movement. The British influence gave western
labour a greater sense of political responsibility and thus made
it a more accommodative force within the community.

Other influences tended likewise to place a sharp brake
upon the radicalism of western Canadian labour. It was
perhaps no accident that the conference at which the O.B.U.
was launched met in Calgary. The spirit of western revolt has
found its fullest expression in this city far distant from eastern
Canadian centres and exposed from the beginning of its history
to strong American influences. Out of Calgary grew in western
Canada the Equity league, the Nonpartisan League, the United
Farmers of Alberta (most militant of early agrarian organizations), the C.C.F. party, and the Social Credit movement.
But western labour as an organized force met its first test of
strength in Winnipeg where, although the working population
was larger than in Calgary, the forces of community conservatism were much stronger. Winnipeg had no important neigh-
bouring urban communities, and it was surrounded by a solid
agricultural population, now two generations old and politically
powerful. In such a situation no really revolutionary workers'
movement could hope to develop. The strikers in 1920 had to
face not only the opposition of an aroused body of local citizens
determined to break the strike but the equally determined
opposition of the rural population.

Nor could the Winnipeg strikers look for much support
from the Canadian community at large. Strikes in Calgary,
Edmonton, Vancouver, Port Arthur, and Toronto, helped to
maintain morale, but there was no large body of radical opinion
to which to appeal. The vigorous intervention of the federal
government and the threatened use of military force were in the

Canadian tradition of calling upon the authority of the state
to suppress any movement which assumed too radical a character.   Influences of geography which favoured the dispersion
of authority were offset by a strong sense of responsibility for
the maintenance of order on the part of the central government.
The toleration by the Canadian population of the use of force,
and its sensitiveness to any act which threatened constituted
authority, placed nonconformist political elements at a serious
disadvantage.   To carry out the general strike, the Winnipeg
labour leaders were forced to constitute themselves a sort of
ad hoc government.   Fifty years earlier in the same western
community Louis Riel and his Métis followers had been forced
into a similar position in seeking to negotiate better terms with
the Canadian government.   Both movements carried a threat
which could not be tolerated by a state such as Canada, with
long lines of communication to defend, and both met with the
decisive intervention of centralized authority.

The Winnipeg general strike, the rise of the Independent
Labour Party, and the joining of the labour and farmer political
movements in the C.C.F. were important phases of the development of the western Canadian political community.   The strike
in Winnipeg drove a wedge between labour and agriculture
which the Calgary conference leading to the formation of the
C.C.F. attempted to remove.   The extent of the success
achieved was evident in the election victories secured by the
new political party in the industrial communities of eastern and
western Canada and in its capture of the government of the
predominantly rural province of Saskatchewan.   Failure, however, was evident in the break-up of the farmers' political movement in Alberta and the rise of the Social Credit party.   Professor Masters' study offers important background material
for the understanding of what happened in Alberta in 1935.
Though the O.B.U.'s experiment with the general strike may
seem very different from the experiment of the Social Credit
party with the national dividend and just price, both were true
expressions of the West's urge to build a better world in which
to live, and both ran so counter to the demands and exactions
of the Canadian federal system that they were bound to fail.

S. D. CLARK

Acknowledgements

I WISH to express my thanks to all who have assisted in the preparation of this book. I am especially grateful to Messrs. R. Durward, William Ivens, J. L. Johnston, the Provincial Librarian of Manitoba and A. J. H. Richardson of the Public Archives of Canada for repeated and courteous help, and to Chief-Justice E. K. Williams and Mr. Isaac Pitblado, K.C., for advice and for the loan of material. I had very useful conversations with Messrs. A. A. Heaps, R. Holmes, R. J. Johns, A. D. Longman, the late A. A. MacDonell, Armour Mackay, Arthur Puttee, R. B. Russell, H. P. Shaw, and F. G. Tipping. Miss Ethel Johns contributed a memorandum and read the first draft of the manuscript. Messrs. R. W. Prittie, W. Pritchard, A. P. Cooper, and Mrs. Gloria Queen-Hughes sent in valuable material.

Permission to reprint the quotation on page 68 from G. V. Ferguson, *John W. Dafoe*, has been given me by the author and by the publisher, the Ryerson Press, and I am very grateful to them.

To my wife, for encouragement, sympathy, and many invaluable suggestions, I owe a debt which I wish to acknowledge but which I can only very inadequately describe.

I am indebted to Professor S. D. Clark, the editor of the series, and to the committee of readers, for sound and constructive criticism, and to the Canadian Social Science Research Council for assisting in the expenses of research and publication.

D. C. MASTERS

Bishop's University
Lennoxville, P.Q.
March, 1949

Contents

Illustrations

THE WINNIPEG GENERAL STRIKE

CHAPTER ONE

Before the Strike

I T W A S on Sunday afternoon, December 22, 1918, that the Socialist party of Canada held its famous meeting in the Walker Theatre in Winnipeg. "Canada's finest theatre" they called it, and on this day it was host to an audience of variegated racial origins—Anglo-Saxon, Polish, Ukrainian, Hungarian, and other. In serried rows they sat gazing at the curtain with its woodland scene, its scroll-work, and urn-shaped motto:

> Finds tongues in trees, books in the running brooks,
> Sermons in stones, and good in everything.

Singularly inappropriate it was in a meeting dedicated to the purpose of finding no good at all in the government.

Soon the speakers appeared on the platform. The crowd cheered and Sergeant Langdale, from Winnipeg military Intelligence, poised his pencil expectantly. John Queen opened the meeting, a canny Lowland Scot, a cooper by trade, shrewd and genial, with a wide circle of friends, always apparently on top of the world. He described the purpose of the meeting with vigour and with a touch of humour. It had been called to protest against the policy of the Canadian government, especially in regard to Russia, and all the leading Winnipeg socialists were present to move the resolutions of protest. Bob Russell was present, another Lowland Scot from the Clydeside, a machinist by trade, only thirty years old, dark and animated, with a colourful Scottish vocabulary. Russell was a leading member of Machinists' Local 122, the moving force in the Metal Trades Council and a most influential member of the Winnipeg Trades and Labor Council. R. J. (Dick) Johns was there, a slight 29-year-old Cornishman; "the boy with a smile," they called him. Handsome and genial, a man's man, who could hold an audience spellbound by his eloquence and his gleaming eye, Johns was a machinist and Russell's colleague in the Metal Trades Council and the Winnipeg Trades and Labor Council. Fred Dixon was there, too, one of the leaders of the Winnipeg labour movement, a fine-looking Englishman with a deep and resonant voice. So was George Armstrong, the real founder of the Winnipeg branch of the Socialist party of Canada. In his middle forties at the time, Armstrong was a member of the Carpenters' Union and an ally of Russell and Johns in the Winnipeg Trades and Labor Council. He was the only native Canadian in the group of Socialist leaders at the meeting. Also present was William Ivens, another Englishman, a former Methodist minister who had broken with his church because of his pacifism and who was now the radical editor of the *Western Labor News*. More picturesque and more indiscreet was beaming Sam Blumenberg, a Jewish member of the Socialist party, conspicuous among his colleagues by his flaming red tie.

The speeches of protest against the government proceeded. Armstrong supported the motion demanding that the government repeal all its wartime orders-in-council. Ivens moved that all political prisoners, many of whom were labour men, should be released. "I am here," he said, "to champion the rights of humanity. The imperial system must go." Fred Dixon seconded the resolution. Russell rose to move the third and final resolution that the Canadian government should send no more troops to fight against the Russians. In his salty Scottish language Russell championed the Russians and social-ism. "Capitalism," he is reported to have said, "has come to a point where she is defunct and must disappear." The crowd applauded and Sergeant Langdale's pencil raced feverishly over the page. Blumenberg got up to second the resolution. "Bol-shevism," he is reported as saying, "is the only thing which will emancipate the working class. . . . There are thousands of men coming back who went over to fight. They will say, 'We have fought for this country and by the gods, we are going to own it.'" The resolution passed amid great enthusiasm.

The crowd left the building quietly and dispersed without any demonstration.[1]

This Walker Theatre meeting was the penultimate event in the train of developments which ended in the Winnipeg strike. One may well enquire how the labour movement had developed that restless, volatile character which much of it appeared to have at this time.

A glance at the history of the trade union movement will indicate that until 1914[2] it had remained comparatively mild and orthodox. Labour organization had commenced in the west during the last two decades of the nineteenth century. Five locals were established in Manitoba during the eighties. By the year 1902 there were fifty-six locals in Manitoba out of a total of 1,078 in all Canada. By 1912, out of 1,883 locals, Manitoba had 139, Saskatchewan 113, Alberta 152, and British Columbia 249. As might have been anticipated, the leadership in the shaping of opinion had been taken by Manitoba and British Columbia, the two more industrialized of the western provinces, Trades and Labor Councils having been formed in Vancouver and Victoria in the eighties and in Winnipeg in 1894. The movement which grew up was, by and large, a conservative trade unionist movement, and its demands were moderate. It is true that throughout the period there was a general lack of sympathy and understanding between the western and eastern branches of the Canadian labour movement. Distance and the pull of geographic and economic forces, together with the comparative immaturity of the western movement, helped to create this breach, and the formal association of western locals and Trades and Labor Councils with the Trades and Labor Congress of Canada did not heal it. It is also true that industrial unionism had created something of a furore in British Columbia in the late nineties, but the crisis had passed. For the most part labour was concerned with

[1]Preliminary hearing, *The King* v. *William Ivens et al.*, testimony of F. E. Langdale. *Manitoba Free Press*, Nov. 29, 1919.

[2]For the western labour movement before 1914, see Harold S. Logan, *The History of Trades-Union Organization in Canada*, Chicago, 1928; *Trade Unions in Canada: Their Development and Functioning*, Toronto, 1948. *The People's Voice*, labour newspaper, Winnipeg, 1894-1914.

wages and hours and its rather mild political activity was directed towards such objectives as compulsory education, municipal ownership of franchises, nationalization of railways, and so forth. None of these demands had the explosive possibilities of the labour radicalism of 1918 and 1919.

Typical of the temper of western labour was the programme put forward by the first Independent Labor Party which was organized in Winnipeg in 1895. It proposed such reforms as the restriction by law of the working day to eight hours, the abolition of overtime and piecework, the nationalization of railways, telegraphs, telephones, and mines, and the municipal ownership of all franchises. Until 1914 western labour was largely unanimous in its belief in orthodox trade unionism and in political activity which showed itself in the running of candidates for the House of Commons, the provincial legislature, and the city council. In 1900 the I.L.P. in Winnipeg elected its first M.P., A. W. Puttee, who won a closely contested by-election against E. D. Martin, an Independent Liberal. The Manitoba Labor Party was formed in 1910. Like the I.L.P., it favoured a programme of constitutional reform. From about 1904 there was a radical minority in Winnipeg and the West which gradually increased in strength. From 1904 to 1918 the Social Democratic party and the Socialist party of Canada functioned in Winnipeg. But the keynote of the period before 1914 was quiet and solid labour organization unaccompanied by much of the radical agitation which was later to create such a sensation in western Canada.

World war came in 1914. As it progressed a new note became apparent in the western labour movement: a vigorous note of protest. Labour was less docile, more impatient with grievances and with the obstacles to their remedy. It had embarked upon a new era characterized by increasing irritation and by more extreme proposals for reform. In this rising movement of protest Winnipeg played a leading part.

Winnipeg in 1914 was a city not very far removed from its frontier origins. Originally a centre of the fur trade, with the opening up and development of the West, it had become a wheat-marketing centre. Thus it was largely a product of the great period of western expansion which commenced shortly after 1896 and ended in 1913. From a population of something over 40,000 in 1901, it mushroomed to 128,000 in 1911. By 1919 it was to reach a total just under 180,000.

The economy of Winnipeg was based upon the export of wheat and the distribution of incoming goods. The city had little heavy industry; local manufactures consisted mainly in the processing of meat, wood pulp, and vegetable products, and in the production of textiles. The labour population was occupied mainly in railway shops, public utilities, the construction industry, processing plants, and light industry.

Although many Europeans had come to Winnipeg after 1900 the city in 1919 was two-thirds Anglo-Saxon. The sixty thousand of "non-British" origin included considerable groups of Ukrainians, Germans, Poles, Russians, Swedes, and Icelanders. Each of the two largest groups, the Ukrainians and the Poles, numbered about six thousand. North Winnipeg had assumed its modern polyglot complexion, although a large influx of central Europeans was still to come in the decade of the 1920's.[3]

Rapid expansion had produced wide variations in wealth, sufficient to attract the notice of the provincial commission, headed by H. A. Robson, K.C., which investigated the strike of 1919. The well-to-do and the less well-to-do, though scattered throughout the city, were, to a considerable extent, segregated in particular areas. The *entrepreneur* and professional classes, mainly Anglo-Saxon, were to be found in Armstrong's Point, Wellington Crescent, and River Heights. North Winnipeg, parts of Fort Rouge, and much of north-west Winnipeg, were inhabited largely by the labour population, of which the "new Canadian" element lived mainly in north Winnipeg.

The western movement of protest, in which Winnipeg assumed the lead, was the product of basic forces which will be described below. Yet the form which it assumed was largely a result of the impact of a group of ardent and able men who harnessed the prevailing discontent in support of certain specific

[3]During the decade of the 1920's, the total population of Winnipeg increased from 179,087 to 218,785, an increase of 39,698, or about 22 per cent. During the same period the total of those of non-British origin rose from 58,518 to 84,331, including 13,209 Germans, 11,228 Poles and 18,358 Ukrainians, and making an increase of 25,813, or about 44 per cent.

proposals of reform. They were all comparatively young, they were all very able, and the level of debating ability in the group was high. Moreover, and this point is central to an understanding of the western labour movement, they were all, with one exception, born and educated in the British Isles. To a considerable extent the course followed by the western labour movement, particularly in its Winnipeg phase, can be explained by the personalities of these men, and may be regarded almost as an extension of the British labour movement.

Perhaps the two most influential members of the group were Russell and Johns. Both had come to Canada before the war, Russell in 1911 and Johns in 1912. Both were machinists, able speakers, and shrewd labour politicians. Both were socialists: Johns a member of the Social Democratic party and Russell a member of the Socialist party of Canada. Both had great influence in the Machinists' Local 122 and in the Winnipeg Trades and Labor Council.

Working closely with Russell and Johns was William Pritchard, who had been born in England of Welsh descent and who was thirty in 1919. Pritchard was distinctly a man of parts: a fine athlete, a musician of ability who organized juvenile orchestras and male voice choirs, an omnivorous reader who, at the age of eleven, had read Josephus and Gibbon. A Marxian socialist, he was a brilliant thinker and his native Welsh fire made him a most eloquent speaker. His speech to the jury in the trial of the Winnipeg strike leaders in 1920 was a classic example of proletarian oratory. Pritchard had been apprenticed to a building contractor in England, but had come to Canada and settled in Vancouver in 1911. During the war years he had assumed a prominent position in the British Columbia labour movement. Here his eloquence and the zest with which he engaged in the rough and tumble of labour politics had stood him in good stead. "As a speaker he enjoys a good fight with a worthy opponent," wrote a contemporary, "but fairly revels in a wordy scrap with an unfair antagonist." The campaign to form the O.B.U. in March 1919 had brought Pritchard into contact with Russell and Johns and resulted in his presence in Winnipeg at the time of the strike of 1919.

A fourth member of this group was George Armstrong, who hailed from Ontario and in 1919 was forty-five years of age. He was a strong socialist. For years he taught socialist classes in Winnipeg and he was the principal founder of the Winnipeg branch of the Socialist party of Canada. He was described by a former associate as a soap-box orator of considerable ability. His talents fitted him to make a popular appeal. He was a very vocal member of the Winnipeg Trades and Labor Council in which he represented the Carpenters' Union.

Russell, Johns, Armstrong, and Pritchard may be regarded as composing a distinct group. All were socialists; all favoured the formation of the O.B.U.; and all worked closely together, the first three in the Winnipeg Trades and Labor Council and all four in the O.B.U. Sympathetic towards the members of this group, but less closely associated with them, were three other prominent labour leaders: John Queen, A. A. Heaps, and William Ivens.

Perhaps the most dynamic and certainly the most charming of these was John Queen of Lanarkshire, who had come to Canada in 1906. In 1919 he was thirty-six years of age. He early became a socialist and a member of the Social Democratic party. He is chiefly remembered now as having been seven times mayor of Winnipeg and a perennial member of the Manitoba legislature, but that came later. In 1918 he was already an alderman, having been elected to the council in 1916. Queen was a big man physically and of a genial, pleasant personality. He had a great gift of humour which often rescued him from embarrassment. Later in the legislature his flashes of wit made the house forget the cross-fire of debate when he was in danger of being backed into a corner. He had a quick mind and a great deal of political sagacity. He was unequalled in his ability to appraise the effects of a piece of legislation. He was essentially a humanitarian and advocated his principles with remarkable consistency throughout a lengthy career.

Queen, as a member of the city council, was a valuable spearpoint of labour influence. He was joined on the council in 1917 by A. A. Heaps, born in Leeds of Jewish extraction, who had taken a considerable interest in the British labour movement before coming to Canada in 1910. In 1919 Heaps was thirty-four years of age, a furrier by trade, a member of the Winnipeg Trades and Labor Council as well as an alderman and a member of the Social Democratic party. While perhaps not as dynamic as Queen or Johns, Heaps was thorough, conscientious, and shrewd. He combined effectively with the more colourful Queen in the advocacy of labour interests.

A third important ally of the Russell-Johns group was William Ivens, the first editor of the *Western Labor News*. Ivens, born at Barford in Warwickshire, had come to Canada in 1896 at the age of eighteen. After a brief career as a market gardener, he had entered the University of Manitoba as a candidate for the Methodist ministry. He had been ordained in 1908 and had continued on circuits until 1918. His pacifism during the first world war and his advocacy of social reform had turned him against the Methodist Church, and in 1919 he was expelled from the ministry because of his refusal to accept another ministerial appointment. He had already become editor of the *Western Labor News* in 1918. He was a vigorous humanitarian, an excellent organizer, and an eloquent apologist of labour both in the press and on the platform. Like some of his associates, he had transferred to the cause of social reform all the emotion and idealism which he had formerly devoted to preaching the gospel. He had less grasp of political realities than some of his colleagues but a great capacity for appealing to the imagination.

Such were the individuals who helped to guide the destinies of the Winnipeg labour movement. The term group can be applied to them only with reservations. All were sympathetic to labour and all were socialists, but all were not members of the same party. Russell and Armstrong and Pritchard belonged to the Socialist party of Canada. Johns and Queen and Heaps were Social Democrats, members of a party which sought to achieve much the same ends as the Socialist party but by more constitutional means. Four of the seven were associated together in the O.B.U. movement, while three were not. There were also the inevitable differences in temperament, which no doubt led to differences in policy. The eloquent Johns presented a striking contrast to the shrewd and canny

Queen or the able though colourless Heaps. Seven important individual labour leaders they were, but scarcely a homogeneous group.

The western radicals had worked, during the war, in an atmosphere of increasing labour unrest which stemmed from many causes: rising prices which had got more and more out of line with wages, conscription, war measures restricting freedom of speech, the attitude of the government and of many Canadians to Russia after the November revolution of 1917. The war crisis of 1917-18 had temporarily diverted the farmer from concentration on domestic grievances, and the Union Government had captured 41 out of 43 prairie seats in December 1917. But this simply confirmed western labour in its opposition to government policy. Under the impetus of its grievances the labour movement in Manitoba, and in the West generally, became more belligerent and in many quarters less satisfied with the methods of orthodox trade unionism. Radical labour men showed a distressing tendency to cry "Strike" or even "General strike" upon the slightest provocation. At times they resembled the Queen of Hearts in *Alice in Wonderland:* they were always crying, "Off with their heads!"

Indicative of the prevalent labour unrest was the series of strikes in western Canada in 1918. Of these the most serious occurred in Winnipeg. It lasted for over three weeks and reached semi-general proportions. In some ways it was a rehearsal for the general strike which began a year later. The strike originated in the civic services of Winnipeg. The employees in the city light and power department, who had demanded increased wages and who refused to consider a bonus, went out on May 2, to the number of 90.[4] On May 3 the city electricians and waterworks employees struck. They were followed by the teamsters on May 7, the firemen on May 14, and the telephone operators, who were employees of the province, on May 16. On May 21 four thousand railway workers (machinists, moulders, blacksmiths, etc.) struck, and on May 22 the street-cars stopped running.

Opinion in labour circles was not unanimous in support of the strike. This is indicated by the attitude of *The Voice,*

[4]*The Voice,* May 3, 1918. For chronology of the strike see *Winnipeg Telegram,* May 25, 1918.

published by the moderate A. W. Puttee. On May 17, it described the action of the unions as "too precipitate," and continued, "The *Voice* believes that there is a time to strike, but that time is after all efforts of conciliation and arbitration have failed."

However, a great deal of sympathy was expressed for the strike in the Winnipeg Trades and Labor Council where Johns, in a characteristic utterance, asserted "The time is not for compromise. . . . You have the right to demand anything that you have the power to enforce. In the City of Winnipeg we have the might, let us use it."[5]

The committee directing the strategy of the strike felt strongly about the alleged treachery of *The Voice* and published its own paper, the *Labor News*. The *News* vigorously insisted that the strike was entirely justified.[6] So strong was labour opinion that the Trades and Labor Council actually considered the calling of a general strike but had not acted when a settlement was reached.

The course of the strike was punctuated with repeated efforts at a settlement. The first of these occurred after appointment by the City Council, on May 9, of a committee to negotiate with the strikers. The proposals of this committee were reported to the council by Controller Puttee on May 13.[7] It was a conciliatory report providing for various increases to the waterworks operators, electrical workers, firemen, and other civic employees.

Unfortunately the prospects of an immediate settlement were wrecked by an amendment introduced by Alderman Fowler and passed by a vote of nine to eight. The Fowler amendment raised the highly controversial issue whether employees in public utilities had the right to strike. It was a question which was being hotly debated in 1918 and which was destined to emerge again during the great strike of 1919. It was the basic issue in the famous Boston police strike of June 1919. The Fowler amendment denied civic employees the right to strike. It proposed that all persons employed by the city should express

[5]*The Voice*, May 17, 1918.
[6]*Ibid.*, May 24, 1918.
[7]*Ibid.*, May 17, 1918.

their willingness to sign an agreement "undertaking that they will not either collectively or individually at any time go on strike, but will resort to arbitration as a means of settlement of all grievances and differences."

It soon became obvious that no settlement was possible so long as the Council clung to the Fowler amendment. The labour representatives on the Council, Queen, Heaps, and Puttee, all opposed the amendment with great vigour and no little asperity. This alliance of radical and moderate labour on the Council was indicative of the attitude of labour in general in Winnipeg towards Mr. Fowler's reservation. All were agreed that it deprived the civic employees of a fundamental right.

In this view labour was supported by the federal minister of labour, the Hon. Gideon Robertson, who descended upon Winnipeg, a veritable *deus ex machina*, and ended the strike. Robertson's influence was conciliatory and decisive. Having arrived on May 23 he immediately urged the City Council to abandon the Fowler amendment. "He himself was of the opinion," reported the *Winnipeg Telegram* of May 23, "that the committee's report would give satisfaction to the men if the council removed from it the restriction on the right of the men to withdraw from the service of the corporation when they believe that the provocation warrants them in doing so."

Robertson's intervention was well timed because it followed conversations between the strikers and the citizens' committee of one hundred. The citizens' committee was an *ad hoc* body of purportedly neutral citizens, mainly business men and lawyers, formed to negotiate a settlement. Its role in the 1918 strike was very different from that of the similar and larger citizens' committee of 1919. Unlike its successor, the committee of 1918 negotiated directly with the strikers. As a result, A. L. Crossin, one of its members, reported to the Council that the strikers and the committee had reached agreement on every point except one, whether officers of the fire brigade should be included in the union.[8]

This single obstacle was soon removed, and on Friday, May 24, the City Council negotiated the settlement. The unions of the civic employees were reorganized, modified wage

[8]*Winnipeg Telegram*, May 25, 1918.

schedules were accepted, and the right to strike was allowed as a legitimate weapon, in the last resort.   All future disagreements were, however, to be submitted to a board of arbitration.   On the vexed question of officers in the fire brigade, the strikers conceded the point; the officers were not to be in the union.[9]

The settlement represented, on the whole, a victory for labour.   Not only had wage schedules been revised upwards, but the City Council had been forced to abandon the principle of the Fowler amendment.   Labour had been successful largely because of its allies, the minister of labour and the citizens' committee.   The strike and its outcome had an unfortunate influence on the attitude of many labour leaders in Winnipeg. As a labour man said to the author, "They thought that if they said 'Boo' the boss would run."   This led to an aggressive truculence which was an important influence in precipitating the general strike of 1919.   Too little account was taken of the importance of labour's allies of 1918 and too much emphasis attached to the might of Winnipeg organized labour.

A serious crisis had been overcome in May 1918 but the record of strikes in western Canada in that year was only beginning.   In July the centre of unrest shifted westward to British Columbia where a strike of employees in the British Columbia Electric Railway Co. paralysed transportation in Vancouver, North Vancouver, Victoria, and New Westminster. The strikers demanded an eight-hour day, with pay ranging from forty cents per hour up to fifty-one cents, according to length of service.[10]

Later in the same month a second crisis developed in Winnipeg, this time in the metal trades, which were an area of continuous unrest from 1917 on.   Most of the metal workers were employed in the railway shops and were organized in nineteen craft unions.   These unions were all represented in a central body organized in Winnipeg and known as the Metal Trades Council.   Most of the Council's constituents and its officers were employees in the railway shops.   However, it also represented the so-called contract shops.

[9] *The Voice*, May 31, 1918.
[10] *Ibid.*, July 5, 1918.

The contract shops were independent firms which filled contracts as distinct from the railway metal shops which were parts of a larger concern. The three largest were the Vulcan Iron Works, the Dominion Bridge Company, and the Manitoba Bridge and Iron Works. The contract shops were the Balkans of the Winnipeg labour world. They were always in a state of unrest and always likely to precipitate a strike which could spread to the railway shops and perhaps even farther.

The men claimed that wages in the contract shops should be raised to the height established for the metal workers in American railways by the famous McAdoo Award.[11] In addition, they claimed recognition for the Metal Trades Council. On June 1 the Metal Trades Council presented demands for higher wage schedules to the contract shops.

In July this dispute was to flare up into a hard fought and bitter strike which lasted for over a month. Two issues were involved, wage schedules and recognition. The proprietors of the three largest contract shops had always been firm in their attitude towards organized labour. On this occasion their objection to higher wage schedules was strengthened by the realization that acceptance of the demands from the Metal Trades Council would involve its tacit recognition. Such recognition the proprietors shunned like the plague. They insisted that they would deal with their own men but not with a body which was composed mainly of railway employees. They ignored the submission of the Metal Trades Council. The Dominion government appointed a royal commission to investigate the dispute, but irate employees were exasperated to learn that it was not empowered to make recommendations, and they decided to strike. They went out on July 22.[12]

From the beginning it was a bitter struggle, which became even more acrimonious after the employers secured from the Manitoba courts an injunction in restraint of picketing. The metal trades secured enthusiastic support from the Trades and Labor Council and many of the delegates agreed "that the

[11]The award which was made by William G. McAdoo, director-general of the American railroad administration, was followed by increases on the Canadian railroads of 15 per cent in March, 1918, and 25 per cent in the following August (*Canadian Annual Review*, 1920, 328).

[12]Western Labor News, Aug. 2 and 9, 1918.

labor movement could not now keep out of the fight, and see the Metal Trades workers go down to defeat, through an order granted by our courts."[13] On August 15 the Council resolved to call upon the affiliated unions to take a strike vote, and a general strike would probably have been called had not the dispute been settled before completion of this vote. Returns after a week of voting showed the overwhelming count of seven to one in favour of a general strike.[14] Thus for a second time in 1918 this drastic measure had been proposed. It was an ominous portent.

The dispute in the metal trades was gradually settled by piecemeal negotiations between the various contract shops and their own workmen. There was no general agreement. Nineteen of the smaller firms had negotiated settlements by August 23. In the following week agreements were announced between the three large contract shops and their employees.[15] By August 29 the strike was over.

The immediate crisis had passed but the basic cause of unrest, the dispute over recognition of the Metal Trades Council, was not removed. In each case the settlement had been negotiated by the management and by a committee of the employees. The men had seen fit to accept this method of settlement. Yet further disputes over recognition, as well as over wages, were still on the cards.

Even this did not end the story of strikes in western Canada in 1918. In October a dispute began in Calgary between the C.P.R. and freight handlers who claimed the increase brought in by the McAdoo Award should have been paid from May 1 instead of from August 1. They also protested about the appointment of a foreman who, it was alleged, had been promoted over the heads of twelve other possible candidates. As a result the Calgary freight handlers struck and precipitated a strike of C.P.R. freight handlers from Fort William to Vancouver. The Edmonton Trades and Labor Council endorsed

[13]*Ibid.*, Aug. 16, 1918.

[14]*Ibid.*, Aug. 23, 1918. *Manitoba Free Press*, Aug. 23, 1918.

[15]*Manitoba Free Press*, Aug. 26, 27, and 30, 1918. Settlements were announced by the Dominion Bridge Company on Aug. 26, the Manitoba Bridge and Iron Works on Aug. 27, and the Vulcan Iron Works and two small firms on Aug. 29.

this action and the Calgary Trades and Labor Council ordered a general strike vote.[16]

Once more there was talk of a general strike in Winnipeg. On October 18 the *Western Labor News* announced that the executive of the Trades and Labor Council had taken the initial steps. Wires were sent to Ottawa, to the strikers, and to various Trades and Labor Councils. "The one note that was clear," said the *News*, "was that, if necessary, a general strike of the whole Dominion would be called in defiance of the order of the government." This time the pro-strike majority was even more overwhelming. On October 25 the Trades and Labor Council announced that the ballots so far counted were in favour of the general strike by a vote of twelve to one.[17] Only just in time was a tentative settlement of the Calgary dispute announced. On the same day, October 25, the *Western Labor News* reported that all the Calgary strikers had been reinstated with the exception of twenty-five whose fate was to be considered by a board of adjustment.

The strike record of 1918 was extremely alarming, indicating growing labour unrest. Not only had there been serious and bitter strikes in Winnipeg, Vancouver, and Calgary, but opinion in support of a general strike had developed.[18] Such action by labour threatened to tie up the whole western economy.

The unrest so prevalent in the ranks of western labour had its repercussions in the Winnipeg Trades and Labor Council where a sharp struggle developed between two groups: the orthodox, rather conservative trade unionists and the more radical element led by Russell and Johns. Typical members of the trade unionist group were F. G. Tipping, Ernest Robinson, James Winning, and H. Veitch. In general they approved of the existing system of trade unions, which they regarded as well

[16]*Western Labor News*, Oct. 11, 1918.

[17]*Ibid.*, Oct. 25, 1918.

[18]It has been suggested to the author that in Winnipeg alone was there much support for a general strike. This was not so. Not only did the Calgary Trades and Labor Council order a general strike vote but at the Calgary convention of March, 1919, resolutions calling for a general strike were submitted by the B.C. Federation of Labor and by the Brule (Alberta) local of the United Mine Workers of America, and the idea was given much support by delegates from centres other than Winnipeg.

designed to improve the position of labour. They envisaged no fundamental reconstruction of society, but instead orthodox efforts to raise wages and reduce hours within the framework of the system of capitalist free enterprise.

The so-called radicals were impatient with trade union methods which they regarded as too slow and too accommodating to capital and the government. They objected also to the divisions in the ranks of labour which organization into separate unions created. They favoured a more unified organization (later they called it the One Big Union) which would consolidate labour as an effective fighting force. As the Walker Theatre meeting was to show, they were extremely critical of the dominion government for its anti-Russian policy, its failure to release political prisoners after the cessation of hostilities, and its retention of many wartime orders-in-council. Some of these political opinions were shared by the moderates, but the radicals were more active in making protests through mass meetings.

No precise correlation can be established between moderate or radical opinion and particular industries; but it should be noted that some of the machinists, led by Russell and Johns in Local 122, were particularly restless and radical in their thinking. Several reasons for this may be suggested. In the contract shops the machinists had had a long tradition of unsuccessful negotiations with their employers and had no particular reason for continuing to adhere to the system of craft unions. In the railway shops where relations with their employers had been better, they felt the responsibility of improving the lot of their fellows. Furthermore a large proportion were recent immigrants from the British Isles from which some of them brought a radical attitude towards labour policy. As members of a skilled and highly paid group, machinists might have been expected to be cold to radical politics and industrial unionism, and eventually they assumed these conservative attitudes, but this swing had not come in 1919, and the machinists were the stormy petrels of the Trades and Labor Council. However, one cannot explain the entire radical movement in Winnipeg in terms of the radicalism of this group of workers. They provided the leadership, but the Winnipeg delegation at the Calgary convention in March 1919, made up entirely of radicals, represented twenty-six unions as well as the Trades and Labor Council.

The struggle between the two opposing groups flared up in several dramatic clashes in the Trades and Labor Council. The first of these culminated in the resignation of F. G. Tipping from the presidency, after a vigorous attack by his radical opponents. Tipping had been appointed to the royal commission which investigated the dispute in the metal trades in July and August. He signed the report of the commission although it made some recommendations not entirely acceptable to the metal trade employees, such as a maximum rate of thirty-two and a half cents an hour for men engaged in certain branches of the trade.

For signing the report Tipping was vigorously attacked in the Trades and Labor Council by Russell and his associates who claimed that he should have put in a dissenting opinion. Tipping asserted that the issue should not be raised in the Council because he had been appointed to the commission as a member of the carpenters' union, which was presumably neutral in the dispute, and not in virtue of his presidency of the Council. He claimed the right to report first to the Metal Trades Council as the body most directly concerned with the dispute. This the majority of the Trades and Labor Council refused to allow, and on September 5 a vote calling for his suspension was passed by 49 to 10.[19] His resignation was accepted on September 19.[20]

The Tipping incident did not raise any basic issues in dispute between moderates and radicals. However, it provided the excuse for a concerted radical attack on a leading moderate and the result was an impressive radical victory.

A second clash, which was much closer to basic issues, occurred in the Council on January 23, 1919. A proposal had been made earlier in January to organize another mass meeting of labour men in the Walker Theatre to protest against various policies of the dominion government. The meeting would no doubt have been similar in tone to the Walker Theatre meeting of December 22, 1918, which has been described.[21] Members of

[19]*Western Labor News*, Sept. 6, 1918. *Manitoba Free Press*, Sept. 6, 1918.
[20]*Western Labor News*, Sept. 20, 1918.
[21]*Ibid.*, Jan. 24, 1919.

three political parties, Socialist, Social Democratic, and Dominion Labor, had all supported the proposal in the Council, and a committee had been appointed to organize the meeting. Eventually the management of the Walker Theatre refused to rent its premises and the meeting fell through.

The result was a stormy scene in the Council on January 23 in which the radicals denounced Secretary Robinson for allegedly sabotaging the meeting. The inference was that the moderates did not want a mass meeting since it would involve strong expressions of radical opposition to the government. The debate brought out most of the leaders on both sides. George Armstrong blamed Robinson and another moderate, Barlow, for the collapse of the project. Russell strongly supported Armstrong and denounced the officers of the Council. "When the Trades Hall, as well as the Theatre was refused for this meeting," he declared, "there was some reason." Johns in a particularly lurid speech backed up Russell and predicted dramatically, "In Germany the workers were shooting each other down. In Winnipeg tonight we are fighting with ideas, but we shall soon be fighting with rifles."

The moderates replied with equal vigour. Delegate Hoop inferred that the whole project was unwise because it would have associated the Council with political parties. Robinson denied that he had sabotaged the meeting and was supported by Barlow, who actually proposed that Armstrong be expelled for a year from the Council because of his attack on the secretary. Finally, James Winning, who had succeeded Tipping as president of the Council, attempted to quiet the storm by a more conciliatory speech. He asserted, however, that the primary responsibility for the meeting lay with the Socialist party which had decided to go ahead on its own responsibility despite the appointment of a committee by the Council.

There the matter rested. The debate of January 23 was not decisive, but it was significant in clarifying party lines in the Council. The two elements were obviously mutually antipathetic. Neither was in a position to dominate the Council. Contrary to some preconceived ideas, it would be inaccurate to say that the radicals ever completely dominated the Trades and Labor Council in the period prior to the general strike of

1919. The moderate trade unionists were able to maintain considerable strength. When Tipping resigned in September 1918 he was replaced by the equally moderate James Winning. When the general strike came in May 1919 it was precipitated by a union of radicals and moderates. It is true, however, that from about September 1918 the radicals were very much on the offensive in the Council where they were able to exercise a considerable influence.

Outside the Council they were able to disseminate their opinions by control of the newly established newspaper, the *Western Labor News*, which succeeded *The Voice*.[22] *The Voice* had been critical of the strike of civic employees in May of 1918, and this defection many labour men and especially the Russell element could not forgive. The strikers had published the *Labor News* and on June 20, 1918, the Trades and Labor Council resolved to publish its own paper, the *Western Labor News*. Since it was obvious that the labour world in Winnipeg could not support two papers *The Voice* sold out and published its last issue on July 26. William Ivens was elected editor of the new paper and under his vigorous direction the *News* became an exponent of radical labour opinions. It was to be in the forefront of the struggle during the next year and the official mouthpiece of the strike committee during the 1919 strike.

There were many arenas for the expression of radical opinion in western Canada, but the culmination of the whole movement was the attempt to form the One Big Union. The O.B.U., as its name indicated, was conceived as a super-colossal industrial union which would include the entire labouring class and which would, therefore, involve the abandonment of existing craft unions.[23] The organization of the O.B.U. was begun at a convention of the western labour radicals held at Calgary in March 1919.

The philosophy on which the O.B.U. was based can be examined with profit because it indicates how derivative was western labour radical thought. In this perhaps it was not very different from other aspects of Canadian culture. Even a brief description of the O.B.U. opinions will sound a number of

[22] *The Voice*, June 21, July 19 and 26, 1918. *Western Labor News*, Aug. 2, 1918.
[23] *O.B.U. Bulletin*, Nov. 8, 1919.

notes familiar to the student of proletarian history in western Europe and the United States.

The advocates of the O.B.U. assumed, like Robert Owen, Marx, Veblen, and many others, that there were in reality only two classes of society, "those who possess and do not produce, and those who produce and do not possess."[24]   The conception of three classes, the producer, the consumer, and the public, they held to be fallacious.[25]   The O.B.U. was built upon the idea of a social order composed of two elements, workers and non-workers, between which runs a sharp line of cleavage.[26] The professed object was to organize the workers, whether manual or white-collar, into a single union.[27]   Many non-manual workers, said William Cooper, a writer in the *O.B.U. Bulletin*, were inoculated with the views of personal success and were "still working and hoping for a notch higher in the social scale."   This difficulty, he said, must be overcome. There was need in the O.B.U. for both groups: those who worked with their hands and those who worked with their brains.[28]

The question of whether the O.B.U. should enter politics engaged the attention of its advocates.   They were extremely sceptical of the ultimate value of labour's efforts to improve its position by electing members to parliament.   They felt also that, since politics was basically a struggle for power, it was more important to concentrate on the formation of the one big union.   Once that was done, it was maintained, labour would have the power in any case.   There was never any doubt that the movement was intended to have political significance eventually.   "The position therefore is," wrote Cooper, "that we have to use our organization to secure the conquest of political power in order that the control of industry shall be brought into our own hands."[29]   That was the long-run objective.   In the short run, according to the *O.B.U. Bulletin*, the workers could be left in the old political affiliations because it was easier to persuade them to join the O.B.U. than to change

[24]*Ibid.*, Jan. 10, 1920.
[25]*Ibid.*, Dec. 27, 1919.
[26]Logan, *The History of Trades-Union Organization in Canada*, 411.
[27]*O.B.U. Bulletin*, Jan. 10, 1920.
[28]*Ibid.*, Dec. 27, 1919.
[29]*Ibid.*, Oct. 11, 1919.

from one political party to another. Meanwhile the work of education could be carried on. Once the workers were educated in class consciousness and once the movement was soundly established, old party affiliations would mean nothing anyway.[30]

Such was the philosophy of the O.B.U. It represented a point of view which had had its advocates for some time in western Canada. The first annual convention of the B.C. Federation of Labor at Victoria in 1911 had endorsed the principle of industrial unionism,[31] and similar resolutions were passed by all succeeding conventions of the Federation down to 1918. In 1911 the Calgary Trades and Labor Council endorsed the same principle. Such views, which eventually found expression in the O.B.U., will sound extremely familiar to anyone already acquainted with the industrial unionism of Great Britain, France, and the United States.[32] The O.B.U., although less militant, was like the American organization, the I.W.W., and no doubt owed something to American inspiration.[33] Its philosophy was strongly infused with Marxism, particularly in its basic tenet, the class struggle. O.B.U. Marxism was probably derived in part from British industrial unionism which had been heavily influenced by Marx. Its advocates were consciously moved by the example of Russia which was supposed to be a working model of Marxism. "The Soviets are Trade Councils in reality," wrote Cooper in the *O.B.U. Bulletin*, "a new form of political machinery. All this looks like the constituent basis of the One Big Union. In essentials it is the same."[34] Yet the promoters of the O.B.U. were essentially in

[30]*Ibid.*, Sept. 13 and 20, Dec. 27, 1919.

[31]*Ibid.*, Nov. 8, 1919.

[32]There have been three types of industrial unionism: two concerned with the organization of all the workers in a single industry, the other favouring "one big union" including all workers of all industries (John R. Commons, *History of Labor in the United States*, New York, 1918, II, 533-5).

[33]There was an important difference in organization. The I.W.W. grouped its workers according to industries and then united them in a central organization, while the O.B.U. grouped them according to the territories in which they worked. In small towns all the workers were organized in a single unit. In large centres separate units could be formed for each industry, according to the wish of the workers. In each city all the units were under a central labour council which controlled O.B.U. affairs in its district. (M. D. Savage, *Industrial Unionism in America*, New York, 1922, pp. 186-201.)

[34]*O.B.U. Bulletin*, Dec. 13, 1919.

the British tradition of industrial unionism. To be sure there had been some interaction between British industrial unionism and the I.W.W. and the *syndicats* in France in the early years of the twentieth century.[35] Among the leaders of British industrial unionism, Tom Mann had encountered the I.W.W. in Australia and had become imbued with the O.B.U. idea. James Connolly, another leader of the movement in Great Britain, had spent seven years (1903-1910) in the United States where he had worked closely with the I.W.W. It was the British movement with which the O.B.U. promoters had been in immediate contact. Industrial unionism had had a considerable history in Great Britain as will be shown by a consideration of the Grand National Consolidated Trades Union of the 1830's, the Social Democratic Federation of the eighties, and the careers of Connolly and Mann between 1910 and 1914.[36] Russell, Johns, Queen, Ivens, and Pritchard, all were immigrants from Great Britain and were no doubt strongly influenced by British thought. Russell came from the Clydeside where industrial unionism had secured its firmest hold and where it lingered after having lost ground in other parts of Great Britain.[37] A particularly important member of the Winnipeg group and probably the source of most of its ideas was William Cooper who wrote a number of impressive articles on the philosophy of the O.B.U. in the *Bulletin* in 1919 and 1920.

Cooper had had a long career in the English trade union movement. He was a cabinet-maker in Aberdeen and took an active part in the carpenters' union which staged a nine weeks' strike in the early nineties. Later he became interested in politics and was one of a small group which formed the Aberdeen

[35]Sidney and Beatrice Webb, *The History of Trade Unionism*, London, 1926, pp. 654-5.

[36]As in other parts of the world, industrial unionism and syndicalism were associated in Great Britain. Industrial unionism has been defined as advocating the inclusion in one union of "all who work in an industry, skilled and unskilled, regardless of difference in craft, sex or race" (Savage, *Industrial Unionism in America*, 3). Syndicalism has been described as "a revolutionary Labour movement making the trade unions the basis of social revolution as well as of future society" (*The Penguin Political Dictionary*, London, 1939). The leaders of the Grand National Consolidated Trades Union and of the S.D.F. of the eighties, and Connolly and Mann before 1914, were all syndicalist and industrial unionists.

[37]Webb, *The History of Trade Unionism*, 658-9.

branch of the Social Democratic Federation. During this period of his life he came into contact with such socialists as A. M. Hyndman, Tom Mann, Harry Quelch, Bruce Glazier, G. Aveling and Mrs. Aveling, who was a daughter of Karl Marx. For eleven years he was a member of the Aberdeen City Council and during the latter part of this period was chairman and convenor of the public health committee. He was one of a group on the council who succeeded in placing the tramway system under municipal control and in erecting workmen's dwellings.

Cooper came to Winnipeg in 1907 and was employed as a cabinet-maker, at first by the C.P.R. and later by the C.N.R., for which he worked for twenty years. With his background and experience in the British labour movement he was a valuable accession to the Socialist party in Winnipeg. His work in the party consisted mainly in writing and lecturing. He was a well-read man and had taken pains to master the English language during his early days in Aberdeen. He used to be fond of saying that the telling is of as great importance as the subject itself and that even if people will have nothing to do with your ideas they may be attracted by the way in which you relate your story. He wrote extensively in *The Voice* and later in the *Western Labor News* and the *O.B.U. Bulletin.* He also conducted a Workers' university on Monday afternoons which was attended by many active in the labour movement including J. S. Woodsworth and William Ivens. Cooper was a man of wide influence in advanced labour circles in Winnipeg and his British background helps to explain the similarity between British industrial unionism and the philosophy of the O.B.U.

Many parallels can be shown between the ideas of the O.B.U. and the British tradition from which it was largely derived. Basic to the whole O.B.U. position was the idea of uniting all the workers, skilled and unskilled, in a single immense union. The idea reached far back in the history of the British labour movement, beginning with the Grand National Consolidated Trades Union. The Social Democratic Federation of the eighties and nineties, of which Cooper had been a member, was based upon the same idea. H. M. Hyndman, its leading member, stated in 1887:

The day has gone by for the efforts of isolated trades. . . . We appeal therefore earnestly to the skilled artisans of all trades, Unionists and non-unionist alike, to make common cause with their unskilled brethren, and with us Social-Democrats, so that the workers may themselves take hold of the means of production, and organize a Co-operative Commonwealth for themselves and their children.[38]

The same idea of a union of all workers in a single union was central to the thinking of industrial unionists such as Connolly and Mann early in the twentieth century. Connolly, for instance, said:

Natural law leads us as individuals to unite in our craft, as crafts to unite in our industry, as industries in our class, and the finished expression of that evolution is, we believe, the appearance of our class upon the political battle-ground with all the economic power behind it to enforce its mandates.[39]

There were of course variations between some of these schemes and the O.B.U. plan. Owens and Connolly, for instance, envisaged organization by industries with, at the top, as the connecting link between them all, a national union or federation. The O.B.U. envisaged a more complete fusion of workers in all industries at the level of local branches of the organization. Yet the essential idea of one huge national union comprising all the workers was present in all these schemes.

It is also possible to cite many British examples of the idea that the workers should perfect a thorough economic organization before engaging in political activity, and that political control would follow almost automatically. Owen had regarded political democracy as quite secondary to economic democracy.[40] James Connolly put it even more clearly. The function of industrial unionism, he said, was "to build up an industrial republic inside the shell of the political State, in order that when that industrial republic is fully organized it may crack the shell of the political State and step into its place in the scheme of the universe."[41] Tom Mann described the same objective in vigorous language in 1911:

[38]*Ibid.*, 410.
[39]*Ibid.*, 656.
[40]*Ibid.*, 154.
[41]*Ibid.*, 656.

Finally, and vitally essential it is to show that economic emancipation to the working class can only be secured by the working class asserting its power in workshops, factories, warehouses, mills and mines . . . and wherever work is performed, ever extending this control over the tools of production, until, by the power of the internationally organized Proletariat, capitalist production shall entirely cease, and the industrial socialist republic will be ushered in, and thus the Socialist Revolution realised.[42]

Also basic to the philosophy of the O.B.U. was the division of society into two classes only: the exploiters and the exploited, the capitalists and the workers of all kinds. From the days of Robert Owen, who had classified society into the "idle" and the "industrious," this dual conception had had great vogue in the English working-class movement. There can be no doubt that so far as Cooper, Russell and others were concerned, the immediate source of this, as of the other ideas in the O.B.U. philosophy, was the thinking of industrial unionists who had crossed the seas; and they were not of the stuff of which communists are made. Like their British counterparts they could talk Marxist jargon with great fluency, but they were not in the Russian revolutionary tradition. None of the O.B.U. leaders became communists in the years after 1919. This was a result not so much of advancing years as of innate moderation, an essential part of their British heritage.

On the front page of the *Western Labor News* of March 7, 1919, appeared a cartoon in which a fat, repulsive-looking capitalist was wooing a winsome female named Labor Union. The lady carried a work-basket labelled *Strike* while from Capitalist's pockets protruded papers marked *Capital, Lower Wages,* and *Profits.* Cooed the capitalist, "Let us unite, dearest! Our interests are identical." The coy charmer meanwhile remarked *sotto voce,* "The Old Hypocrite! He's as wily as a serpent. But wait till I get him."

This quaint little picture was typical of the tone of western labour radicalism in the winter of 1918-19. It was replete with protests—protests against the Canadian government, against Capitalism and against the intransigence of eastern Canadian labour for refusing to desert its craft unions. The western

[42]*Ibid.,* 658.

Canadian labour world was in a ferment and there was developed the atmosphere out of which emerged the Calgary convention and later the Winnipeg general strike.

The proposals of labour radicals took two forms in 1918-19. The first was political and consisted in protests against the policies of the government on conscription, censorship of the press, and Soviet Russia. The second was non-political, the reorganization of labour itself into a more effective union structure.

The political protests do not bear directly on the proposal to form the O.B.U., but they helped to create the atmosphere of unrest in which it developed. A number were made in British Columbia in 1918. In August the Vancouver Trades and Labor Council called on all its affiliated unions to stage a twenty-five hour strike in protest against the shooting of a man named A. Goodwin by the police at Cumberland, B.C. Goodwin, a former vice-president of the B.C. Federation of Labor, had taken to the woods when called up for military service and was later shot when attempting to escape from the police. "What we want to know," exclaimed William Pritchard, "is if the military authorities, in the round-up of evaders, will shoot a man on sight for his labour activities."[43] In January of 1919 another political protest came from the coast when Local Union 2299 of the United Mine Workers of America at Cumberland passed a resolution protesting against the federal government's prohibition of entry into Canada for books published by the Charles M. Kerr Publishing Company of Chicago, "our main source of the classics of working class philosophy."[44]

In Winnipeg the *Western Labor News* published a number of articles and editorials defending Soviet Russia and the dictatorship of the proletariat. "There are men, real men," said the *News* on September 20, 1918, "who believe that there is something in Bolshevism that is essential to a free democracy and to civilization." On January 10, 1919, after describing extensive unemployment in Winnipeg, Toronto, and other cities, the *News* predicted, "Unless these things change with almost lightning rapidity we shall find that Bolshevism will not confine

[43]*Western Labor News*, Aug. 16, 1918.
[44]*Ibid.*, Jan. 24, 1919.

itself to Russia, Austria, Germany, Spain and the Balkans. Will Ottawa ever wake up?" The socialist column of the *News*, in a flaming article published on January 24, predicted the dictatorship of the proletariat. "When the workers take control," threatened the writer, "they will form a Dictatorship which will give the same order to the owners of the world that Lenin gave to the capitalists of Russia: Obey or starve!"

Extreme statements like the above were certainly not typical of western labour as a whole. Yet they indicate the penchant of western radicals for wild talk which was not borne out by their subsequent attitudes and activities. Such utterances increased the excitement in western labour circles and also, as appeared later, thoroughly alarmed the general middle-class public.

The leading incidents of the period of political protest were the two mass meetings in Winnipeg: the Walker Theatre meeting of December 22, 1918, which has already been described, and a second meeting, also sponsored by the Socialist party of Canada, but held at the Majestic Theatre on January 19, 1919. Russell, Johns, and Armstrong were present again at this second meeting, attacking capitalism and advocating socialism. That the meeting had political overtones is suggested by the testimony of B. T. Battsford, later a witness at the preliminary hearing of the strike leaders in 1919. Russell, he said, "went severely after the press and pulpit and censorship, and said the truth had not been told about Russia. . . . He was supporting the Soviet Government of Russia against the attacks of the press and pulpit and organized propaganda throughout the world, against it."[45]

The Majestic Theatre meeting had a significant sequel. At its conclusion the chairman, Rees, announced that there would be a memorial service in the Market Square on January 26 for Karl Liebknecht and Rosa Luxemburg, German socialists who had been killed in the post-war struggle for control in Germany. This service never took place owing to the intervention of a considerable number of returned soldiers. The soldiers were understood to declare that they would prevent a service to

[45]Preliminary hearing, *The King* v. *William Ivens et al.*, testimony of A. Edward Reames, B. T. Battsford.

commemorate Germans.   Many of them were concerned also
with the problem of re-employment and resented the fact that
so many jobs were held in Winnipeg by "aliens."   This resentment against the "aliens" was an important element in the
unrest in Winnipeg which preceded the outbreak of the general
strike.   To a large extent it accounts for the behaviour of many
returned soldiers during the strike.[46]   On the occasion of the
abortive service of January 26, about two hundred returned
men, marching together, entered the Market Square, openly
stating that they were looking for the speakers at the meeting.
Very discreetly no speakers appeared.   Afterwards the soldiers
carried on considerable rioting directed apparently against
aliens.[47]   This went on sporadically for two days. Sam Blumenberg's cleaning establishment on Portage Avenue was wrecked.
The soldiers also staged a demonstration in front of the Swift
Packing Company against the employment of aliens, but were
persuaded by Mayor Gray to disperse and allow the management to handle the problem.   The January riots petered out.
Yet they were significant because soldier parades, as will appear
below, played a decisive part in the history of the general strike
of 1919.

While western radicals rang the changes in political protest
they had also begun the series of economic proposals which
culminated in the inauguration of the O.B.U.   The most important statement of western industrial unionism, and one
which had far-reaching repercussions, occurred at the annual
convention of the Trades and Labor Congress of Canada which
met at Quebec in September 1918.   The Quebec convention
brought into the open the clash of views between western radicalism and eastern trade unionism.   A direct result was the subsequent calling of the Calgary convention.

The western delegates, representing Vancouver and Winnipeg and other cities, were largely though not entirely radicals,
and included Russell and Robinson from Winnipeg and Jack
Kavanagh, a Vancouver delegate whose opinions were similar
to Russell's.   They introduced a series of resolutions designed
to secure acceptance by the Congress of the western radical

[46]*Ibid.*, testimony of Capt. F. G. Thompson.
[47]*Ibid.*, testimony of Sergeant Edward Reames.

programme. Most significant were those which expressed criticism of the craft unions and which called for a more general industrial organization. The principal resolution from the Winnipeg Trades and Labor Council proposed that the Congress "take a referendum vote on the question of reorganizing the Canadian labor movement into a modern and scientific organization by industry instead of craft." Winnipeg also sent a resolution calling for a six-hour day and a five-day week and a resolution asking for representations to the minister of justice to release political prisoners to work on farms. The Vancouver Trades and Labor Council sent a resolution charging the government with using the power of the state in the interests of the employer and with buying labour officials with government jobs. The resolution called for an amendment to the constitution of the Trades and Labor Congress making government appointees ineligible for office in the Congress.

Much to the dismay of the western delegates these resolutions were all snowed under by the votes of eastern trade unionists. Russell and Kavanagh were particularly disgusted with the Congress and with eastern labour in general. "Considerable education is needed in the East," said Kavanagh loftily, "and it is up to the Western workers in their own interests to see that they get it."

A most significant development followed this setback. The western delegates concluded that western labour must secede from the Trades and Labor Congress. At the conclusion of the Quebec convention they held a separate meeting and made plans for the calling of a western conference. A committee was appointed with David Rees of Vancouver, international organizer of the United Mine Works of America, as chairman and V. R. Midgley of the Vancouver Trades and Labor Council as secretary. The committee issued invitations to trades and labour councils and labour unions in the West inviting them to send delegates to a convention of western labour. Such was the origin of the movement which led to the Calgary convention.[48]

Prior to the holding of the convention in March of 1919, radical leaders, in Vancouver, Calgary, and Winnipeg, en-

[48]Logan, *The History of Trades-Union Organization in Canada*, 372-6. *Manitoba Free Press*, Aug. 30, 1918. *Western Labor News*, Oct. 4 and 18, 1918.

deavoured to popularize the O.B.U. type of organization. Russell and Johns and Armstrong in Winnipeg, Kavanagh and Pritchard and E. E. Stevenson in Vancouver, and Joe Knight in Edmonton, were among the most active.

Excerpts from the correspondence which passed among this group were introduced as evidence at the trial of the strike leaders in Winnipeg. They indicate their attitude and the nature of their activities. Russell wrote to Knight: "Well, Joe, I expect we will now be confronted with the horrors of peace and it is to be hoped that the Reds [Russell's usual term for labour radical] will wake up now and get in all the propaganda that can be expounded twenty-four hours per day."[49] Russell also spoke of the coming convention and reported assurances from David Rees "that B.C. are solid for the thing and so is Saskatchewan and Manitoba." In Alberta he reported more opposition especially from Ross, a Calgary trade unionist. In a second letter to Knight, Russell reported that British Columbia and Manitoba were solid for the O.B.U. and appealed to Knight to "pull off the stunt in Alberta."[50] The correspondence also brought out Russell's opposition to the Dominion Labor party which he regarded as a futile exponent of working-class interests. "The movement here is developing rapidly," he wrote to E. E. Stevenson on January 3, 1919, "we are fast knocking hell out of the Labor Party." This salutary process apparently continued, as Russell reported to Stevenson on January 25, "At a meeting of the Trades and Labor Council [of Winnipeg] we had a great victory, and killed the labor party for sure."[51]

The Calgary convention was worked up by an active minority which organized this conference," said a delegate at the convention.[52] While the leaders were corresponding and urging each other to renewed efforts, they were making a good deal of progress in their respective provinces.

The movement in Winnipeg culminated in a meeting of the Trades and Labor Council on March 9 at which a series of

[49]*Manitoba Free Press*, Dec. 1, 1919, *The King* v. *R. B. Russell.*
[50]*Ibid.*
[51]*Ibid.*, Dec. 2, 1919, *The King* v. *R. B. Russell.*
[52]*Winnipeg Tribune*, April 5, 1919. The speaker was V. R. Midgley of Vancouver.

resolutions was passed in general support of the position which was to become that of the O.B.U.[53] The Council resolved that a referendum vote of all affiliated crafts be taken on the question, "Are you in favor of scientifically reorganizing the workers of Canada upon the basis of industrial organization instead of craft unionism?" The Council also resolved upon the appointment of a Central Industrial Committee to function in any disputes that might take place in the West and specified that representatives be elected according to industries.

In Alberta the O.B.U. movement early in 1919 became sufficiently pronounced to engage the attention of the police, and Sergeant Waugh of the R.N.W.M.P. began to investigate the socialist and O.B.U. advocates.[54] Later, in March and June, he attended a number of meetings in support of the O.B.U. His investigation threw a good deal of light on radical labour activities in the province. Organized labour in Alberta consisted chiefly of miners, railway employees, civic employees in Calgary and Edmonton and other centres, and workers in other urban industries such as carpenters, plumbers and steam-fitters, and hotel and restaurant employees. The United Mine Workers were of great importance because they were large and aggressive. Waugh became acquainted with P. M. Christopher, the president of District 18 of the U.M.W.A., with Ed Browne, its secretary, and with a number of leading members of the U.M.W.A. As in Winnipeg, so in the U.M.W.A., leadership was exerted by recent immigrants from the British Isles. Waugh said of the U.M.W.A., "In the majority they are Russians and Austrians, very few Germans, of Slavic descent. The principal leaders are radical socialist Englishmen." Christopher was an Englishman and Browne was Irish. There were, however, a greater proportion of Europeans prominent in the Alberta movement than in either the British Columbia or the Manitoba movement. Waugh mentioned such men as W. Kolling and Max Stigler, both members of the U.M.W.A., Alderman A. G. Broatch of Calgary, and Carl Berg of Edmonton, who was later a member of the provincial executive of the O.B.U. Despite

[53]*Western Labor News*, March 14, 1919.

[54]Preliminary hearing, *The King* v. *William Ivens et al.*, testimony of Sergeant Waugh.

greater participation by "foreign" elements in Alberta, the leadership was dominantly Anglo-Saxon. Even the U.M.W.A. sent twenty-three Anglo-Saxons to the Calgary convention and only seven "foreign" delegates.

In Alberta as elsewhere in the West the affairs of the Socialist party of Canada and of the proposed O.B.U. were closely related. Joe Knight, for instance, was a socialist and W. McQuoid, the president of the Calgary local of the Socialist party of Canada, was a supporter of the O.B.U. Political protests and proposals for the reorganization of labour, therefore, went together. Early in 1919, District 18 of the United Mine Workers held a convention in Calgary and passed resolutions in favour of the six-hour day and the five-day week, the release of political prisoners and the dispatch of greetings to the Spartacists of Germany and the Russian government. The Socialist party of Calgary continued to hold sessions which combined in their purpose business and popular education. According to Corporal F. W. Zaneth of the R.N.W.M.P., who assisted Sergeant Waugh in his investigation, there was considerable discussion in Calgary socialist meetings about the possibility of a general strike and many opinions were expressed in favour of the Russian system of government.[55] In Edmonton, Carl Berg, who was one of Russell's correspondents, vigorously advocated the O.B.U. which he regarded as a prototype of the I.W.W.[56] Meetings in Calgary on January 26 and February 23, respectively, under the auspices of the Socialist party, passed resolutions favouring the right of free speech, removal of the censorship ban on radical literature, and the abolition of orders-in-council.[57] On March 9, on the eve of the convention, another public meeting was held in Calgary, this time at the Pantages Theatre. William Pritchard was present and speeches were made, according to Sergeant Waugh, praising the Soviet system of government and demanding the overthrow of the capitalistic system. Pritchard and Knight held several meetings in Calgary at this time advocating the O.B.U.

[55]*Manitoba Free Press*, Dec. 6, 1919, *The King* v. *R. B. Russell*, testimony of Corporal F. W. Zaneth.

[56]*Ibid.*

[57]*Ibid.*, Dec. 5, 1919, testimony of Sergeant Waugh.

In British Columbia, which appeared even more vigorous in support of radical labour policies, much organizational work was accomplished during the first two months of 1919. The culmination of the movement was the convention of the B.C. Federation of Labor which met in Calgary immediately prior to the general western convention.[58] The fact that the executive of the Federation decided to move the meetings to Calgary from Victoria, where they were to have been held in January 1919, was in itself significant. The reason for the change was "so that trades and labor councils, labor unions, etc., entitled to send delegates to the B.C. Federation of Labor Convention, could also, if they desired, credential the same delegates for the Western Conference."

Thus the B.C. Federation played Jacobin Club (without benefit of guillotine) to the Calgary convention. The issues raised and the resolutions passed by the Federation were destined to be repeated at the general convention. The Federation went on record as demanding a six-hour day and a five-day week. Also, with but one dissenting vote, it resolved to take a referendum vote of its membership on the proposal to sever its connection with the international unions and to form an industrial organization. That the Federation deliberately threw down the gauntlet to the internationals was evident by the statement which its president, J. Taylor, was described as making, "He realized that in passing this resolution that Gompers would proceed to call the rest of his disciples together and with candle, bell and book excommunicate all his dissenting flock." The convention protested against the sending of troops to Russia, and demanded freedom of speech, of the press, and of assembly.

There was ominous talk of a general strike in western Canada. David Rees insisted that a general strike should be called if the Federation failed to achieve its objectives. Joseph Naylor, a U.M.W.A. delegate from Cumberland, urged that the strike should be started on May 1 instead of June 1 which had already been suggested because, as he said, everybody would be out of work by June and a strike would be impossible. V. R. Midgley of the teamsters, a prominent Vancouver labour

[58]*Calgary Daily Herald*, March 11, 1919. *Western Labor News*, March 14, 1919.

leader, also advocated a general strike. "Personally he did not believe any strike was lost; it showed that there was some resistance in the workers." Another delegate, J. Stevenson of the carpenters, was opposed to any policy of "wait and see" and favoured a strike on May 1. There was some opposition, but the support given the proposal showed that many members of the Federation were in an impatient and belligerent frame of mind. They were to find many kindred spirits in the general Calgary convention.

On March 16, 1919, the Western Canada Labor Conference, commonly known as the Calgary convention, was called to order in Paget Hall.[59] High hopes had been entertained for its success, and the *Western Labor News* spoke for many when it exclaimed, "In Western Canada the new day is dawning. The more effete East is burdensome to the West, and the slavish subservience of parliament to the interests of vested wealth has filled the cup of the West to overflowing." It added hopefully, "The convention will be composed of men with vigour, daring, and undoubted courage."[60] It was probably the largest convention of western labour delegates ever held; its 234 accredited delegates represented all the important and many smaller centres between Port Arthur and Victoria. The largest delegations were from Winnipeg, Vancouver, and Calgary, which sent 47, 50 and 45, respectively. It was a radical convention. Russell, Johns, Pritchard, Kavanagh, and Knight, all were present and dominated the proceedings. None of the leading Winnipeg moderates was present, and there was a similar absence of moderates from other centres.

Another significant fact should be noted. The point has been made that the radical leaders in Winnipeg were dominantly Anglo-Saxon. The personnel of the convention appears to indicate that this was true of the West in general. Of the 234 delegates only 11 had names that were not obviously Anglo-Saxon or Irish and 7 of this 11 were in the Alberta delegation of the United Mine Workers. The Winnipeg delegation did not contain a single "foreign" name.

[59]See *Winnipeg Tribune*, April 5, 1919, for a verbatim report of the convention. A report was also published in pamphlet form by the O.B.U. under the title *The Origin of the One Big Union*.

[60]*Western Labor News*, March 7, 1919.

The opening session began with an address of welcome from R. J. Tallon, president of the Calgary Trades and Labor Council, who was forthwith elected chairman of the convention. Committees of ways and means and of resolutions were set up. Delegate W. Seal's motion that smoking be discontinued was enthusiastically rejected, and the convention proceeded immediately to business with the introduction of resolutions from the various delegations. These were referred to the Resolutions Committee, which subsequently moved a series of resolutions for endorsation by the convention.

Of these the most important laid the groundwork for the organization of the O.B.U., a series of seven resolutions reported by R. J. Johns from the policy committee and passed with little apparent opposition on the first day. The resolutions, in effect, were as follows:

1. The name of the organization was to be "The One Big Union."

2. A committee of five was to be elected to carry out propaganda necessary to popularize the O.B.U.

3. The delegates from each province were to meet and elect a committee of five to work with the central committee.

4. The central committee was to draft and issue a referendum on the question of joining the O.B.U. This was to be submitted to all western trade unions.

5. It was declared necessary in establishing an industrial form of organization to work through the existing councils and district boards.

6. After the returns from the referendum, the central committee was to call a conference of representatives of trade councils and district boards to perfect the plans for the organization.

7. An appeal was to be made to trades councils and district boards for a contribution of two cents per member to finance the educational campaign for the inauguration of the O.B.U.

Several of the speeches in discussion of these resolutions were of significance. Johns, in reference to resolution six, asserted his complete confidence that the craft system was doomed. "We figure it will be an easy proposition," he stated, "as we take it by this the craft line will be eliminated; that is the only thing that keeps it as it is and if you eliminate it, it [the organization of the O.B.U.] will be easy to decide—it will soon be expressed by the rank and file." J. R. Campbell of Vancouver (Carpenters' Local 617) in the same discussion indicated the deliberate comparison which some delegates were drawing between the O.B.U. and the Russian system of government. He referred to the central committee of the O.B.U. as "the central soviet." The provincial committees were "provincial soviets" and so forth.

The delegates voted on the central committee which was called for in resolution two and elected Pritchard, Knight, Johns, Midgley, and Joseph Naylor. All were logical choices since all had played active parts in the movement leading to the convention and in the convention itself. Some regard was also paid to the claims of regionalism since the members came respectively from Vancouver, Edmonton, Winnipeg, Vancouver, and Cumberland, B.C.

The resolutions on the O.B.U. were the constructive phase of the convention's work. Other resolutions, a number of which were introduced by Kavanagh, chairman of the resolutions committee, demonstrated the belligerence of western radicalism and its impatience with the *status quo* and with the policy of the Canadian government. One of these called for freedom of speech, of the press, and of assembly; it further demanded the release of all political prisoners, and the removal of all restrictions and disabilities on working-class organizations, and, sounding the recurrent note, proposed a referendum on the question of holding a general strike on June 1 if these demands were not granted.

The resulting discussion indicated the impatience of many delegates with conventional political action and their desire for more drastic measures. Joe Knight suggested that petitions to the government were pretty useless. What was needed was a more definite class organization which would enable the working man to secure his rights. Delegate R. Sinclair of Vancouver, another immigrant from the British Isles, expressed the same idea. The vote was of no importance, he said. He had been in Canada for fifteen years and never voted. "So far as taking the franchise off let it go so long as we line up conditions alongside the workers and fight." The resolution carried.

Even stronger was another resolution which was carried without discussion. The convention declared "its full acceptance of the principle of Proletarian Dictatorship as being absolute and efficient for the transformation of capitalist private property to communal wealth," and dispatched fraternal greetings to the Russian Government, the German Spartacists and all definite working-class movements in Europe. Among the other resolutions was one demanding a six-hour day and a five-day week and another demanding a general strike on June 1 if Canadian troops were not withdrawn from Russia.

The convention ended on a note of exultation and the delegates dispersed, most of them determined to organize the O.B.U.[61] The convention was important because of its constructive work and because it indicated that western radicals were impatient, belligerent, and willing to precipitate a general strike if the occasion should appear to demand it. The convention further demonstrated that many labour leaders were socialists, that they had a profound respect for the Russian system of government, and that they had lost faith in orthodox political methods.

[61]There was obviously very strong support for the O.B.U. in the convention, with no formal opposition, but C. H. Gardiner of Victoria reported a private discussion among delegates who resolved to oppose the idea when they got home.

CHAPTER TWO

The Strike: First Phase

I T W A S the evening of May 6, 1919, and the atmosphere was tense as the members of the Winnipeg Trades and Labor Council took their places in the drab, low-ceilinged assembly room on the second floor of the Labor Temple. The question to be discussed was whether a general strike should be called in Winnipeg. The building trades employees were out; so were the metal workers. Would the Council support them by calling a sympathetic strike? It was a grave issue and the delegates were solemn, realizing the importance of their decision.[1]

President Winning, Fred Tipping's moderate successor, took the chair and the meeting began. Secretary Robinson read a letter from Tom Moore, President of the Trades and Labor Congress of Canada, informing the Council that he would reach Winnipeg on the following Friday and would be prepared to address a meeting of union workers on Sunday. Many of the delegates regarded Moore as a weak-kneed compromiser in championing the rights of labour before employers and government. His offer was unceremoniously rejected.

Excitement rose when the Secretary read out a note, which had just arrived, asserting that a striking metal worker of German birth named Fickenscher had been arrested for visiting various shops, on the instructions of his local, to "pull out" any men still working. Delegates jumped to their feet and clamoured to go and investigate. A committee was chosen for the purpose and departed. Amid growing tension the meeting awaited their return. Finally the committee came back with

[1]*Western Labor News*, May 9, 1919.

Fickenscher, who had been released. Fickenscher was presented to the meeting, and when it became known that he had to appear in court the next day the Council instructed its lawyer, T. J. Murray, to take up his defence.

Now came the issue of the general strike. Delegate Lovatt outlined the progress of the dispute in the building trades. President Winning spoke firmly in support of the building trade workers. They were striking, he explained, without strike pay because their international had refused to sanction their action. The Council, he felt, must back the strikers. "Labor must show a solid front," declared the president, "and must win."

Winning spoke for the right wing. He was followed by salty Bob Russell who spoke for the left. The time to strike had come, said Russell. There were strikes in many parts of the country. Six thousand builders were out in Toronto. A prominent Winnipeg industrialist was going up and down the country stiffening the opposition of the bosses. "Winnipeg must stand firm," declared Russell amid thunderous applause, "for the sake of labor elsewhere."

H. Veitch, another moderate, counselled a policy of caution. The spirit of labour at this time was tremendously inflammable, he warned, and a conflagration might have great and unforeseen effects. No one listened to Veitch. Instead the meeting decided to take an immediate strike vote in the unions affiliated with the Council. The secretary was instructed that the vote was to be speedy; returns must be in within the week.

The final step was taken by the Council on Tuesday, May 13.[2] It was a crowded meeting and again feeling ran high. "Never before in the history of Winnipeg has there been such a Trades Council session," reported the *Western Labor News*. "It was tense, electric and determined, yet seized with a wonderful gravity. Every inch was jammed with a seething mass of trades unionists, men and women." The meeting proceeded with grim dispatch. Delegate Lovatt reported abortive steps which had been taken by Mayor Gray of Winnipeg to achieve a settlement. Several speakers declared that the demands of the workers were just and could not be denied. Amid an oppressive hush Ernest Robinson got up to announce the result of the ballot. It was

[2]*Ibid.*, May 16, 1919.

overwhelmingly in favour of the general strike. Over eleven thousand had voted aye and only five hundred no. The meeting broke into cheers. It was "unanimously and enthusiastically" decided to call the strike at 11 A.M. on Thursday, May 15.

So came the Winnipeg general strike. To many it must have seemed like a bolt from the blue. The Calgary convention had been succeeded by a period of energetic propaganda for the O.B.U. The central committee was vigorously pushing the referendum.[3] There seemed no reason to doubt that, given a period of comparative peace in the field of labour relations, the O.B.U. would soon become firmly established in western Canada. But it was not to be. Before the O.B.U. was well started, the movement was jeopardized by the Winnipeg strike, which diverted the attention of many radical leaders, eventually landing some of them in jail, and which largely discredited the general policy they advocated.

The crisis which had ended in the strike had been comparatively brief. The first public intimation of trouble came on April 24 when both the building trades and the metal trades employees presented wage schedules to their employers.[4] In the case of the metal trades the dispute was complicated by the refusal of the employers to deal with the Metal Trades Council which claimed to be the bargaining agency for the metal workers. It was a dispute over recognition of the Metal Trades Council as well as over wages.

Various efforts were made to settle the two disputes. On April 28 it was learned that the building trades had conferred with the Builders' Exchange representing the employers. The meeting was abortive and on April 30 the building trades workmen decided to strike. More important in stirring up the general strike was the dispute in the metal trades because of the influence they wielded in the Trades and Labor Council. On May 1 a meeting of all employees concerned in the dispute was held and it was decided to strike. This involved not only employees in the contract shops, where the dispute originated, but also in the railway shops, where there had been no dispute. There followed the meeting of May 6 in which the Trades and

[3]Logan, *The History of Trades-Union Organization in Canada*, 385.
[4]*Manitoba Free Press*, May 15, 1919.

Labor Council decided to take a strike vote of its affiliated unions.

A new method was introduced in the taking of the vote. Voting was to be in the various unions but it was declared that an over-all majority in favour of a general strike would result in all the unions striking whether or not each individual union had a majority in favour of the strike.[5] In the result the provision was unimportant since all the unions supported the strike. Seventy unions voted. In some a meeting was called for the taking of the vote. In others the men voted while at work. The vote appears to have been fairly conducted, according to a subsequent report of H. A. Robson, K.C., who was appointed by the Manitoba government to investigate the strike. Robson questioned members and officers of eighteen unions and reported that even those opposed to the strike "stated that the large majority had voted in favour of such a strike and the figures obtained from these sources substantially agreed with the report made public."[6]

A number of unions not affiliated with the Trades and Labor Council were also invited to strike.[7] Among them were lodges of the Brotherhood of Railway Trainmen and the Brotherhood of Locomotive Firemen and Engineers. Considerable numbers of men in these lodges met in informal meetings and took strike ballots. Many went out on strike. Since this action was unauthorized, their international officers later moved to expel those who had departed from the laws and principles of their respective unions. An abortive attempt was also made by the metal workers to persuade foremen in the contract shops to strike.[8]

Belated efforts were made by Mayor Gray of Winnipeg and Premier Norris of Manitoba to negotiate settlements in the building and metal trades disputes. They convened a con-

[5]*Western Labor News*, May 9, 1919.

[6]*Royal Commission to enquire into and report upon the causes and effects of the General Strike which recently existed in the City of Winnipeg for a period of six weeks, including the methods of calling and carrying on such strike*, report of H. A. Robson, K.C., Commissioner, 14-15.

[7]*Ibid.*, 16.

[8]Preliminary hearing, *The King* v. *William Ivens et al.*, testimony of G. Roche and A. E. Brock.

ference on Monday evening, May 12, of employers and employees in the trades concerned. The conference was continued on the Tuesday afternoon but was unsuccessful.[9] On Tuesday evening the Trades and Labor Council made its fateful decision. The strike was now almost inevitable.

In accordance with the notice issued by the Trades and Labor Council the strike began promptly at 11 on Thursday morning, May 15. Street-cars began to run up "To Barn" signs and headed homewards, dropping passengers on the way. In most cases no new passengers were picked up. By noon practically all the tracks were deserted.[10] A *Free Press* reporter went out to Weston to see the beginning of the strike in the C.P.R shops and reported that the men came out laughing and joking like naughty schoolboys.[11] The C.P.R. shop at Transcona and the Canadian National and G.T.R. shops also became idle. Work was entirely suspended at the post office. Many restaurants shut down immediately. A group of strike leaders repaired to their favourite restaurant for lunch and were surprised to find it closed. At the Venice Café the fifty or sixty employees deserted the boss and his two partners who were compelled to close on the evening of Friday the sixteenth.[12] The telephone girls joined the strike at 7.30 A.M. on Friday. The telegraph operators had already gone out. Elevators ceased to run in most of the city buildings, and the barber shops, except those operated by the owners, closed.

What produced the greatest sensation in the public mind was the failure of the bread and milk companies to deliver on Friday morning. No act of the strikers produced more violent condemnation in the press across Canada. To be sure, deliveries were soon resumed, but this did not save the strikers from the charge of attempting to starve infants and invalids.

During the early stages of the strike between twenty-five and thirty thousand workers went out. This meant for Winnipeg in general no mail, street-cars, taxis, newspapers, telegrams, telephones, janitor service, elevators, barbers, or express, freight,

[9]*Manitoba Free Press*, May 15, 1919.

[10]*Ibid.*, May 16, 1919.

[11]Preliminary hearing, *The King* v. *William Ivens et al.*, testimony of B. T. Battsford.

[12]*Ibid.*, testimony of T. J. Kernahan.

or baggage service. For a time it meant no gasoline, milk, or bread, very little meat, and much reduced restaurant service.[13]

At first the city appeared to take the blow with surprising calm. In its last issue before the printers' strike, the *Free Press* rejoiced, "Winnipeg passed through the first day of the general strike without disorder, and without that tie-up of everything that some feared would make an open store seem an oasis in a desert."[14]

It was an ominous quiet. The crowded streets down town on Thursday evening and the vacant street-car tracks were visible evidence that everything was not so well as it seemed in the community. Occasional excitement was provided by the appearance of fire trucks manned by volunteers who, according to the *Free Press*, spent much of the first night answering false alarms. There had been a rush upon the department stores on Tuesday and Wednesday. Others, especially corner grocery stores, also did a "bargain day" business.

Meanwhile the organization and direction of the strike had been taken up by the labour leaders. It soon became clear that the carrying on of a general strike had many ramifications and required careful handling. In order to meet these problems machinery had to be created. The Trades and Labor Council was too cumbrous a body to direct a strike. *Ad hoc* committees had to be created. The transition period between the beginning of the strike and the creation of more formal machinery was bridged by the functioning of a committee of five consisting of R. B. Russell, John Queen, James Winning, H. Veitch, and J. L. McBride.[15]

The composition of this interim committee indicates the mixed nature of the group who precipitated and directed the strike. Russell and Queen were radicals, although not of the same political party. Winning and Veitch and McBride were orthodox trade unionists. McBride was particularly conservative, a vigorous opponent of industrial unionism and much disliked by radicals both before and after the strike. Winning, like the radical leaders, was an immigrant from the British Isles.

[13]*Winnipeg Evening Tribune*, May 24, 1919.

[14]*Manitoba Free Press*, May 16, 1919.

[15]*Ibid.*, Feb. 11, 1920, *The King v. William Ivens et al.*, testimony of William Percy.

Born in Scotland, he was apprenticed to the bricklaying trade and joined the London Order of Bricklayers in 1902. In England, more of a radical than later, he used to sell Robert Blatchford's *Clarion* and supported the great labour and socialist M.P., Keir Hardie. He migrated to Winnipeg in 1906, where he joined Local One, Manitoba Bricklayers', Masons' and Plasterers' International Union. He soon became prominent in his union and in the Building Trades Council. As already noted he supported the moderates against the radicals in the Trades and Labour Council of which he had become president in September 1918. His appointment in 1918 as a member of the Manitoba Minimum Wage Board, a position which he held until 1941, indicates that he was regarded by the Manitoba government as moderate and sound.

It was this combination of opposites which directed the strike for the first week, using room ten on the second floor of the Labor Temple as its headquarters. At a session of strike leaders on Wednesday afternoon, May 21, this *ad hoc* management was replaced by a more complicated organization.[16] This consisted of an outer and an inner strike committee. The outer, called the general strike committee, numbered about three hundred, representing all the unions and other organizations which were involved in the strike. At the session of May 21 the strike committee nominated the inner body, the central strike committee, which had fifteen members including Winning, McBride, Veitch, Russell, and Robinson, the secretary of the Trades and Labour Council, another moderate.[17] The general strike committee elected its own officers, who included W. H. C. Logan as chairman, W. H. Lovatt as secretary, and R. Durward, a very able Aberdonian and a close friend of William Cooper, as assistant secretary. The general strike committee also nominated sub-committees on finance, organization, credentials, transportation, press, and so on.

There is a marked similarity between the central organization of the Winnipeg strike and the Seattle general strike which had been waged briefly and unsuccessfully between

[16]*Western Labor News*, May 23 and 26, 1919.

[17]The others were Anderson, Pickup, Allen, Flye, Smith, Miller, Lovatt, Shaw, Greer, and Noble.

February 6 and 11, 1919. As in Winnipeg, the Seattle strike was precipitated by a dispute in the metal trades which had appealed for support to the Central Labor Council. The strike was directed by an executive committee of fifteen and by a general strike committee of over three hundred delegates. The larger body organized sub-committees on finance, publicity, tactics, and so on.[18] The similarity between the two organizations is too close to be mere coincidence. There had of course been a great deal of talk in Winnipeg in 1918-19 about a general strike. No doubt the labour leaders in Winnipeg had read with interest and profit of the Seattle organization.

To some extent the nature of the work of the two strike committees in Winnipeg is indicated by the organization. There were a number of areas of direction in which the strike leaders were obliged to function. They must decide what additional unions should be called out on strike. The police, for instance, had voted to strike but had been ordered for the time being to remain at work. It was always a question how long they should continue to do so. There was also the question of what workers should be instructed to return in order to maintain essential services. Though striking unions generally try to avoid a direct challenge to the public, preferring "to manipulate or placate, rather than to threaten or coerce,"[19] this is less true of a general sympathetic strike in which the strategy of the leaders is so to inconvenience the public as to make a settlement necessary on the strikers' terms. The latter was the strategy of the strike leaders in Winnipeg. Nevertheless they were unwilling to precipitate a complete collapse of society within the strike area. Their object was to maintain enough services to prevent such a collapse but at the same time seriously to inconvenience the public. Except for the first day or so, the strike leaders attempted to have bread and milk deliveries resumed, and certain other services such as the telegraph and the sale of oil and gasoline continued on a restricted basis. These emergency services involved decisions to keep men at work and even to order back others who had already struck.

[18]W. H. Crook, *The General Strike, Labor's Tragic Weapon*, Durham, North Carolina, 1931, pp. 529-543.

[19]E. T. Hiller, *The Strike, A Study in Collective Action*, Chicago, 1928, p. 174.

Maintenance of some services involved the strike leaders in continuous negotiation with the City Council. This resulted in a good deal of acrimonious discussion, as will appear later.

The strike leaders also had the task of holding the strikers in line and of keeping them out of trouble. Unlike "typical" strike leaders,[20] the Winnipeg men did not try to keep up morale by organizing parades and mass demonstrations. They did sponsor meetings of strikers in the public parks, but the more lurid types of mass demonstrations they shunned like the plague. The reason is obvious. The leaders knew that parades would inevitably lead to disturbances and that, if disturbances occurred, the strike would be broken. They made every effort to keep the strikers off the streets. Throughout the strike the *Western Labor News* issued a daily strike bulletin, the principal public mouthpiece of the strike committees. The *Strike Bulletin* urged the strikers repeatedly to keep out of trouble. Typical of the policy of the leaders was the advice offered by the *Strike Bulletin* on May 20: "The only thing the workers have to do to win this strike is to do nothing. Just eat, sleep, play, love, laugh, and look at the sun. There are those who are anxious for the workers to do something which would provide an excuse for putting the city under martial law. Therefore, once more do nothing." In the same issue the *Bulletin* asserted, "A fight usually means a strenuous time for all concerned. But our fight consists of doing no fighting." Throughout the strike the leaders continued to advocate passive resistance rather than dramatic but risky demonstrations. It was perhaps inevitable that street disturbances should eventually occur. The strike leaders endeavoured to prevent them and for over three weeks succeeded. Had they pursued a less cautious policy the strike would probably have collapsed much sooner than it did.

A remarkable feature of the Winnipeg strike was the extraordinary morale of the strikers. It was not until the third week in June, five weeks after the beginning of the strike, that any serious divisions in their ranks began to appear. The maintenance of morale was another responsibility of the strike committees. They contrived to hold their supporters in line without the use of any of the symbols frequently employed by strike

[20] *Ibid.*, 87.

leaders such as badges, arm-bands, buttons, pennants, parades, exhibitions, or posed pictures in the labour press. There was little picketing to engage the attention of the strikers. In most of the trades involved, strike-breaking did not become a problem until the last few days of the strike. The commissariat under the supervision of A. A. Heaps provided activity for a number of strikers. The theatres which were allowed to operate provided some diversion. For the most part, however, there was little to do except to attend an occasional meeting in one of the parks or a service of Mr. Ivens' Labor Church or to stay home. To a great extent morale was kept up not by the use of symbols or by group activities but by the labour press, especially the *Strike Bulletin*.

Through the *Bulletin* the leaders built up and maintained a concept of the strike as a peaceful protest by long-suffering workers against too low wages and the obstinate rejection of collective bargaining. "Our cause is just," thundered the *Bulletin* on May 21. "Never has there been such unanimity as to the absolute necessity of settling once for all the two points at issue, namely: (1) The Right of Collective Bargaining and (2) the Right to a Living Wage." Later it quoted with approval the opinion of the Toronto *Star* that the issues in dispute were "wages, hours, recognition of unions, and collective bargaining."[21] Again the next day the *Bulletin* returned to the attack under the heading, "What We Want." "The demands of the strikers," it insisted, "are: (1) The Right of Collective Bargaining. (2) A Living Wage. (3) Reinstatement of all strikers."

Under "What We Do Not Want," were listed: (1) Revolution, (2) Dictatorship. (3) Disorder. It was this appeal to the desire for improved wages and hours which held the strikers together for five long, critical weeks.

The recurrent message of the *Strike Bulletin* was verbally repeated in the public meetings which were held from time to time in the parks, especially Victoria, at the end of James Street near the Labor Temple. "If you will but stand firm for a short time," exhorted Ivens, the ex-minister, in Victoria Park on May 16, "we will bring them cringing on their knees to you

[21]*Western Labor News*, May 30, 1919.

saying: 'What shall we do to be saved?' "[22]   A particularly effective form of public meeting was the Labor Church which was organized by Ivens and which conducted services in various parts of the city.   In their Sunday services Ivens and his associates preached the social gospel and the cause of the workers with a fervour derived, especially in Ivens's case, from evangelical Christianity.   Typical of the Labor Church was the service conducted before a large crowd in the Industrial Bureau on the first Sunday evening of the strike.[23] Ivens opened the service with prayer, and an earnest, closely reasoned address was delivered by James Winning.   "The strike," Winning insisted, "was caused by the inadequacy of the pay envelope to last to the end of the week. . . .   The profiteers refused to recognize the men's organizations, and were unwilling to give him a living wage, though they admitted the justice of his demands." Winning scorned the idea that there would be disturbances. "There is not anywhere on earth a more docile people than the workers of this city," he affirmed; and he advised the workers, "Keep your head cool just because there are those who would like you to lose your· temper."   Russell at the same service began his speech by observing facetiously that it was six or seven years since he had been in a church but that this was a new kind of church where people could express their aspirations. He then explained the policy of the strike committee in keeping the police on the job and in maintaining deliveries of bread and milk. It was a political meeting held in a religious setting.   Similar services were held throughout the strike.   Their tone is well illustrated by the Labour Hymn which was frequently sung:

> When wilt thou save the people, Lord,
> O god of mercy, when?
> The people, Lord, the people,
> Not crowns and thrones, but men.

The strikers had reinforced their belief in the justice of their cause with the concept of divine sanction.

So the work of organizing and advocating the strike continued.   It was perhaps inevitable, but unfortunate from the

[22]Preliminary hearing, *The King* v. *William Ivens et al.*, testimony of William E. Davies.

[23]*Western Labor News*, May 20, 1919.

viewpoint of the strikers, that the publicity was all directed towards labour. No effort was made to reach the general public either in Winnipeg or in rural Manitoba. The strike leaders had no ready means of communication with the general public, and such was the concentration on the strike itself that they never attempted to devise one.

As the strike lengthened a *rapprochement* between labour and the public came to appear more and more unlikely. The days became hotter, the temperature averaging well over 80° during the last week in May; tempers became frayed, and problems which had looked capable of solution came to appear insoluble. "The strike ceased to be an adventure," wrote an eye-witness, "and both sides became more bitter and unreasonable."

To a considerable extent the history of the strike can be told by a survey of what happened in the various trades, public utilities, and other services.

Milk and bread should first be mentioned, since it was over the question of their delivery that some of the hottest controversy of the whole strike developed. In the first flush of success the first strike committee allowed the sudden termination of deliveries of milk and bread. Accordingly there were no deliveries on Friday morning, May 16.

The folly of this step soon became apparent. Not only was there a tremendous outcry from the non-labour part of the public that babies were being starved; it became difficult for the families of strikers themselves to obtain milk. On May 16, therefore, the strike committee reconsidered their decision and attempted to work out a solution which would permit the resumption of deliveries. They began negotiations with the City Council and with the heads of the milk and bread companies.

Deliveries were resumed but under conditions which landed the strike committee in an even hotter controversy. To have put the drivers of milk and bread waggons back in service without some indication that they were not strike-breakers would have been to subject them to the dangers of abuse and possible violence. In order to avoid this, the strike committee issued the famous strike placards which were carried by the milk and bread waggons and announced that they were operating "By

Authority of the Strike Committee." These cards were also given to stores and theatres. The reason for this issuance seems clear. There is no reason to doubt the explanation offered by the *Western Labor News* of May 20: "The permit card gives to stores, rigs, theatres, and employees operating these concerns, and to all interested the assurance that these men are not scabbing on the strikers, but are acting in cooperation with them." "The cards were issued at the request of the Teamsters' Union," said William Percy, one of the strikers at the trial of the strike leaders. "They would not return to work delivering bread and milk unless something was given to them to show that they were not 'scabs.' "[24]

While the reasons for issuing the cards seemed clear, such action led to the perfectly proper charge that the strike committee was assuming functions which tended to make it the *ad hoc* government of Winnipeg. This is the dilemma created by a general strike. It so undermines the whole structure of ordinary society that some direction becomes necessary to ameliorate its worst effects. Yet if that direction, even with the best will in the world, is assumed by a strike committee, it is arrogating to itself the functions of government. The same developments occurred during the Seattle general strike where the executive strike committee, in order to provide for hospital laundry, set aside laundry waggons and provided the drivers with signs and permits.[25] In Winnipeg, the effort to maintain partial postal and telegraph service involved the strike committee in the same dilemma as that arising from the delivery of milk.

Typical of developments in the milk industry was the experience of the Crescent Creamery as described by its manager, James M. Carruthers.[26] His drivers belonged to the International Teamsters', Chauffeurs', Stablemen's and Helpers' Union. Their contract with the Crescent Creamery, which provided for no strike or lockout during the operation of the agreement, was supposed to run from December 1, 1918, to

[24]*Winnipeg Evening Tribune*, Feb. 9, 1920, *The King* v. *William Ivens et al.*, evidence of William Percy.

[25]Crook, *The General Strike, Labor's Tragic Weapon*, 536.

[26]Preliminary hearing, *The King* v. *William Ivens et al.*, testimony of James M. Carruthers.

November 30, 1919. However, Mr. Carruthers was notified on May 15 that his men were going to strike. At 11 A.M. all the men in his employment, except some drivers and teamsters out on their rounds, ceased work. Carruthers was left with only eight or ten men. The day's supply of milk soured and had to be dumped. Some milk in cold storage was sold to anyone who came to the creamery and many came. "I must say there was a lot of inconvenience," testified Mr. Carruthers, "in fact, there were pitiable conditions."

In order to redress the situation a meeting was held at twelve o'clock noon at the City Hall on May 16.[27] This was attended by a committee of the City Council, including Queen, Fisher, Hamlin and Fulford, by a committee of the strike leaders, including Veitch, Russell, and Winning; and by representatives of the bread and milk companies: Carruthers of Crescent Creamery, Steinkopf of City Dairy, and Parnell and Milton of the bread companies. Representatives of the hospitals were also present, and one of them has given the author a vivid impression of the strike leaders: "There was no arrogance in the bearing of these men, but there was about them a quiet determination and an air of conscious power that I can never forget. The reins were in their hands and they knew it."

At this meeting, which was convened, adjourned, and reassembled at 2.30 P.M., the strike committee, according to Mr. Carruthers, proposed the partial delivery of milk and bread, but on terms which were not acceptable to the creamery proprietors. Eventually, after the matter had been referred to a sub-committee of the meeting, the strike leaders agreed to allow the drivers to deliver milk in the ordinary way. Carruthers, who had previously taken steps to stop deliveries of milk from the farmers to the Crescent Creamery, immediately advised the railways to inform their agents along their lines that shipments of milk might be resumed. Deliveries of milk began again in Winnipeg on May 18.[28] Milk deliveries were resumed to the hospitals immediately after the meeting of May 16. A representative of the Children's Hospital wrote to the author:

[27]For the account of this meeting see the testimony of Carruthers and also of Mayor Gray, preliminary hearing, *The King* v. *William Ivens et al.*

[28]*Western Labor News*, May 20, 1919.

"When I returned to the hospital I found that the milk had already been delivered, escorted by a guard of apologetic strikers."

The experience of the bread companies was similar to that of the milk companies.[29] Edward Parnell, proprietor of a bread company, testified that on May 14 he received a notification from P. Korns, the agent of Local 34, that the men were about to strike. On May 15 only ten men out of 120 reported for work and deliveries were accordingly suspended. Parnell attended the meeting at the City Hall on May 16 at which it was agreed that deliveries should be resumed. On May 17 the men came back to work but drivers refused to go out with bread without cards on their waggons. Deliveries, with cards on the waggons, were resumed on May 18.

In regard to restaurants the story varies. Some closed completely. Others, like the Venice Café, were operated on a reduced scale. The strike committee attempted to keep as many as possible open, and agreements were worked out with a number according to which the restaurants were to keep open on condition that they were allowed to get supplies. However, some of the restaurants whose proprietors had agreed to stay open eventually closed. This the *Western Labor News* of May 21 interpreted as part of an effort to starve the workers into submission. The *News* warned that hunger is a sharp thorn and that, "The workers must watch themselves at this point and restrain themselves under all provocation."

The experience of the ice companies was similar to that of the milk and bread companies. Charles H. McNaughton, managing director of the Arctic Ice Company, testified that his men went out on May 15.[30] He was informed by the strike committee on May 16 that he could supply the hospitals. Later he was allowed to fill an order for the Grand Trunk owing to the passage of troops through the city. Later still he was allowed to send ice to a few restaurants including the Kensington and the C.V. Café which presumably were *persona grata* with the strike com-

[29]Preliminary hearing, *The King* v. *William Ivens et al.*, testimony of Edward Parnell.

[30]*Ibid.*, testimony of Charles H. McNaughton. *Winnipeg Evening Tribune*, Feb. 20, 1920, *The King* v. *William Ivens et al.*, testimony of Charles H. McNaughton.

mittee. McNaughton testified that he visited the Labor Temple in regard to ice for the restaurants. He saw Mr. Tripp, secretary of the union and, as a result, a few restaurants were added to the list. Meanwhile he was selling ice at the ice-house to anyone who came for it. On May 22 the men returned and the waggons were sent out, bearing, of course, the placards of the strike committee. The Arctic then carried on business with all alike until the men went out again on June 4. McNaughton's evidence was largely corroborated by William MacRury, secretary of the Consumers Ice Company.[31]

Another area of controversy was over the control of gasoline and oil. The strike committee's policy was again one of attempting to regulate operations. Some gasoline stations were closed at the beginning of the strike. Alexander Fraser, who ran a gasoline station at Portage and Kennedy, testified that his business was shut down on May 16 and that "strikers" closed and locked his pumps.[32] Afraid to continue, he remained closed for several days. Ira T. Peacock, manager of the Canadian Oil Companies Ltd. reported that he had been ordered to close his station at Portage and Maryland.[33] Other managers reported similar intimidation. Albert Edward Lewis, manager of the Prairie City Oil Co., which had four stations in the city, reported that some of his men had been intimidated and that one station had been closed for a couple of hours by a stranger.[34] To what extent this intimidation represented the formal policy of the strike committee and to what extent it was simply the action of individual enthusiasts is not clear.

At any rate, on May 18, the strike committee attempted a more moderate policy.[35] The gasoline and oil companies were advised to supply all farmers with coal-oil necessary to meet their requirements and "That Military, Police, Doctors, Health

[31]*Manitoba Free Press*, Mar. 2, 1920, *The King* v. *William Ivens et al.*, testimony of William B. K. MacRury.

[32]*Winnipeg Evening Tribune*, Feb. 21, 1920, *The King* v. *William Ivens et al.*, testimony of Alexander Fraser.

[33]*Ibid.*, testimony of Ira T. Peacock.

[34]Preliminary hearing, *The King* v. *William Ivens et al.*, testimony of Albert Edward Lewis. See also the testimony of James Alexander Boyd, Manager of the Imperial Oil Company in Winnipeg.

[35]Circular "To the Oil Companies Ltd.," from the Winnipeg Trades and Labor Council, May 18, 1919.

Officers, and Hospital Cars must be supplied with the necessary gasoline for Professional Services." The strike committee however required that drivers operating in the industry must have special permits from the strike committee. The oil companies protested against this notice and, according to Mayor Gray, they at first decided to discontinue the sale of gasoline.[36] However, they reconsidered this decision and on May 22 the *Free Press*, which managed to issue a "bulletin," its first publication since May 16, reported that all the gasoline filling stations in the city had reopened.

In accordance with its desire to keep the strikers off the streets and out of trouble the strike committee undertook to keep the theatres open. The experience of the Dominion Theatre was typical. On May 15, according to Bernard Blume, one of its proprietors, the operators walked out. Later the theatre was instructed to open at 5 or 7 o'clock and Davis, the manager, was given a card indicating that he was operating "by authority of the strike committee." This sign he kept up for three or four days. Then the provincial government instructed all the theatre managers to remove the signs under threat that their licences would be cancelled. Accordingly Davis took down the sign. However, his operators, except for their initial departure, remained at work for the first three weeks of the strike.[37] Elmer Jernberg, manager of the Province Theatre, testified to the same effect except that he reported having used a slide which shone upon the screen, "Working in Harmony with the Strike Committee."[38]

In the field of communications the strikers effected a pretty complete cessation of normal activity. This included the post office, the newspapers, telephones, telegraphs, express companies, the street railway, and delivery services.

In the postal service the paralysis was, at first, practically complete. P. C. McIntyre, the Winnipeg postmaster, testified that on May 15 about 400 employees, out of a total of between

[36]Preliminary hearing, *The King* v. *William Ivens et al.*, testimony of Mayor Gray.

[37]*Ibid.*, testimony of Bernard Blume.

[38]*Winnipeg Telegram*, Feb. 24, 1920, *The King* v. *William Ivens et al.*, testimony of Elmer Jernberg.

450 and 500, struck.[39] Carriers, as they came in that morning, threw down their bags and left. Contractors' employees engaged in carrying mail between the railways and the post office also struck. So did transfer men who shifted the mail from one train to another or from one railway to another.

The post office became demoralized. Mail could not be sorted for city delivery, nor could it have been delivered anyway. For ten days business was at a standstill. Postal stations were closed except for one at the C.P.R. station which McIntyre tried to keep open. He was forced to wire the department at Ottawa to stop the dispatch of all but first-class mail to Winnipeg from Montreal, Toronto, and other large cities.

In the telephone, telegraph, and express services the tie-up was at first complete. George A. Watson, chief commissioner of Manitoba Telephones, testified that the day men struck on the evening of May 15, the night room and plant men the next morning.[40] The operators, he recalled, left at 7:30 on Friday morning, May 16. The public service was accordingly discontinued and the city was absolutely without telephone service for a week. Later the telephone strike was extended and on Sunday, May 25, the central strike committee reported that every telephone operator in the whole province had been pulled out.[41] It may be doubted that every operator struck but a sufficient number did so to produce loud protests from the rural areas, as will appear below. The breakdown in telegraph communications was described by J. M. Marshall, assistant manager of C.P.R. telegraphs.[42] Marshall reported that only twenty minutes' notice was given before the operators went out. Two operators, Reeves and Wheaton, representing the others, presented a verbal demand that messages handled by the company be limited to such urgent, non-commercial matters as sickness or death, in which case a sufficient number of operators would be allowed to return to work for this purpose. This

[39]Preliminary hearing, *The King* v. *William Ivens et al.*, testimony of P. C. McIntyre.

[40]*Ibid.*, testimony of George A. Watson.

[41]*Western Labor News*, May 26, 1919.

[42]*Manitoba Free Press*, Feb. 13, 1920, *The King* v. *William Ivens et al.*, testimony of J. M. Marshall.

proposal Marshall rejected, presumably because he was unwilling to accept any regulation from the strike leaders. It was the same dilemma as had arisen in the case of milk. Again the effort at ameliorative measures involved the strikers in exercising or trying to exercise powers which were properly those of government. In the case of the Great North West Telegraph Company this assumption of control by the strikers went further. J. G. Favis, an officer of the company, testified that the strikers had left four operators to handle messages in regard to death, movements of returned soldiers, important military matters, and so on. He produced telegrams stamped by the Trades and Labor Council and initialled by members of the strike committee including John L. McBride.[43] Like the telephones and the telegraph, the express companies were also tied up. William M. Gordon, superintendent of the western division of the Dominion Express Company, reported that all his employees struck with the exception of one or two executives.[44] When 205 employees went out it became impossible to handle any business into or out of Winnipeg. Railway baggagemen also struck.

Other communications were completely or partially paralyzed. The street cars stopped running on May 15 and did not resume until nearly the end of the strike. Cartage and delivery service, carried on in some cases on an individual basis, was never completely suspended, although severely hampered. Howard Munnion, driver of an Eaton delivery waggon, said that on one occasion when he and his partner were delivering on Sherbrook Street a hostile crowd unhitched the horse and dumped the contents of the waggon into the street. Munnion walked the horse for some distance and then mounted in an attempt to escape. Unfortunately the horse became frightened. Munnion fell off and was struck by a flying hoof. It required three weeks in hospital for him to recover.[45] Similarly, W. H. McCullough, the driver of an Eaton truck, testified that a crowd stopped the truck and cut his tires.[46]

[43]Preliminary hearing, *The King* v. *William Ivens et al.*, testimony of James Gibbs Favis.

[44]*Ibid.*, testimony of William M. Gordon.

[45]*Manitoba Free Press*, Feb. 25, 1920, *The King* v. *William Ivens et al.*, testimony of Howard Munnion.

[46]*Ibid.*, testimony of W. H. McCullough.

In the various municipal services (police and fire protection, sanitary inspection, and waterworks) the story was one of varying degrees of breakdown. The police were from the beginning in an anomalous position. They voted in favour of the strike but remained at work on the instructions of the strike committee. Naturally relations between the police force and the city council were strained from the beginning of the strike.[47]

The story of fire protection is part of the story of the citizens' committee, which later will be traced in greater detail. The regular members of the fire brigade struck at 11 on May 15 and were immediately replaced by a volunteer force of 350.[48]

Garbage collection terminated abruptly when the strike began and as it proceeded the cans became fouller and fouller, especially in apartment blocks. Mayor Gray described the situation in a masterpiece of understatement when he said "it made a condition that was not at all nice."[49] Douglas Little, a city sanitary inspector, asserted that there was actually danger of contamination from uncollected refuse, although no one was able to prove that such contamination had occurred.[50]

In the city waterworks the strike committee left a few employees at work with the agreement that pressure should not be above thirty pounds which they considered sufficient for domestic use. Such a pressure was not capable of pumping water higher than the second storey of a building. Consequently those people in offices or apartments above the second floor (few of whom were strikers) were unable to get water.[51]

The returned soldiers did not play a part of very great prominence in the early stages of the strike. Later they were to be a decisive factor in shaping its course; there was little sign of this before the end of May.

Both sides in the strike made efforts to secure support from the soldiers. The *Western Labor News* of May 20, for instance, urged that all members of labour unions who were also veterans

[47]Preliminary hearing, *The King* v. *William Ivens et al.*, testimony of J. K. Sparling.

[48]*Ibid.*

[49]*Ibid.*, testimony of Mayor Gray.

[50]*Manitoba Free Press*, Feb. 26, 1920, *The King* v. *William Ivens et al.*, testimony of Douglas Little.

[51]Preliminary hearing, *The King* v. *William Ivens et al.*, testimony of Mayor Gray.

should attend the next meeting of the Great War Veterans' Association in order to secure the dismissal of the executive, which was declared to be unfriendly to labour, and the election of a more amenable executive. At the same time the returned soldiers were also being urged to support the citizens' committee which had been organized to carry on such public services as the fire brigade and the waterworks. One of the witnesses at the trial of the strike leaders testified that it was as the result of a meeting for returned soldiers held in the auditorium on May 23 that he later enrolled in the special police force.[52]

Neither party in the strike captured the official support of the returned men. The G.W.V.A. always retained its official neutrality. Three delegates, Comrades Law, Bathie, and Moore, were given seats on the strike committee on May 20; but they were there simply in the capacity of observers watching the interests of the returned soldiers and did not give any active support to the strike.[53] The Imperial Veterans Association was even cooler towards the strikers. H. B. Willing, its secretary-treasurer, reported that a delegation of the strike committee urged upon him on May 16 that the association should support the strike.[54] Willing accordingly called a meeting which was advertised in the *Strike Bulletin* of May 17. The meeting, said Willing, "unanimously turned down and refused to have anything to do with the labor side or the citizens' committee." The Army and Navy Veterans, while expressing gratification at being invited to send delegates to the strike committee, refrained from doing so because of the impossibility of calling a special meeting of the association on less than six days' notice. They did offer to call such a meeting if the strike committee desired it, but nothing seems to have come of the offer.[55]

The reason for this official neutrality towards the strike was that the soldiers themselves were divided in their attitude. Those with a labour background supported the strike, and the

[52]*Manitoba Free Press*, Mar. 2, 1920, *The King* v. *William Ivens et al.*, testimony of H. Robinson.

[53]Preliminary hearing, *The King* v. *William Ivens et al.*, testimony of Fred William Law. *Western Labor News*, May 20, 1919.

[54]Preliminary hearing, *The King* v. *William Ivens et al.*, testimony of H. B. Willing.

[55]*Western Labor News*, May 20, 1919.

others were either indifferent or actively hostile. F. W. Law, secretary of the G.W.V.A., explained it thus: "When you have an association composed of possibly 37 per cent employers and 57 per cent of employees and the other 15 per cent of different classes, if you take any stand other than neutrality you are going to make enemies in the association."[56]

The returned soldiers who wanted the G.W.V.A. to support the strike were, said Law, "returned workmen on strike." They had been union men before proceeding overseas and came back to the union. The most notable example of the truth of this statement was R. E. Bray, a returned soldier who played a prominent part on the general strike committee. Born in Sheffield, England, Bray entered the butcher trade and was a constant attendant at labour and socialist meetings. For six years he was a Methodist lay preacher but became a socialist after the discovery "that Christianity was not the means of correcting social injustice." He migrated in 1903 to Winnipeg, where he entered the meat business. Although professedly a pacifist, Bray enlisted in the Canadian army in 1916 because, as he explained, he had "no job and a large family." Having returned to Winnipeg after the war he was simply continuing in the labour tradition to which he had adhered throughout his active career.

On one question the returned soldiers were pretty unanimous and that was in their hostility to "alien" workmen. This hostility had already led to disorders in January 1919 and it was a factor which still had to be taken into account. Law represented the typical attitude of the returned men when he said:

The alien has been one of our first objects you might say, since the return of the men; and knowing, as you say, that these men have been holding down good jobs while our men have been overseas, that is the position of the returned soldier, from the first man who came back, and that is the same today. We are opposed to the alien and will be opposed to him until such time as he gets out of the country, and I am [informed] by labor men themselves that they want him out of the country.

[56]Preliminary hearing, *The King* v. *William Ivens et al.*, testimony of F. W. Law. Law's percentages add up to 109, but his general meaning is clear.

From the beginning of the strike the returned soldiers occupied a position of great strategic importance because they were an element which would make possible the use of force on either or both sides. The essentially reactionary attitude of the soldiers as a result of army discipline might have been expected to fit them for the role of strike breakers *par excellence*, but a labour background had produced in many of them a sympathetic attitude towards the strikers. Whichever attitude they took, whether one of the Right or of the Left, it seemed likely it would be extreme. Such is the usual role of veteran groups, for instance the Independents and the Levellers in the Army at the close of the English Civil War, the anti-South and anti-North groups of veterans after the American Civil War, the part of the Italian army which supported Mussolini in 1922. The tendency of the soldiers to assume extreme positions was, from the first, an explosive element in the strike and one likely to make a peaceful solution difficult if not impossible.

In 1909 came the beginning of what F. L. Allen has called "The Big Red Scare."[57] It was a time when American and Canadian employers saw foreign agitators under every bed. The American employer, said Allen. . . .

had come to distrust anything and everything that was foreign, and this radicalism he saw as the spawn of long-haired Slavs and unwashed East-side Jews. And, finally, he had been nourished during the war years upon stories of spies and plotters and international intrigue. He had been convinced that German sympathizers signalled to each other with lights from mountain-tops and put ground glass into surgical dressings, and he had formed the habit of expecting tennis courts to conceal gun-emplacements. His credulity had thus been stretched until he was quite ready to believe that a struggle of American labouring-men for better wages was the beginning of an armed rebellion directed by Lenin and Trotsky.

Allen wrote of the United States. Yet his description was equally applicable to Canadian employers and, in considerable part, to the neutral sections of the Canadian public.

While these fears were no doubt exaggerated, a series of unfortunate incidents in the United States showed that they

[57] F. L. Allen, *Only Yesterday*, Penguin Books, 76 ff.

had some basis in fact. On April 28 the Red-baiting mayor of
Seattle, Ole Hanson, found in his mail an infernal machine
which failed to explode. Senator Thomas R. Hardwick of
Georgia, chairman of the immigration committee of the Senate,
had attempted to exclude Bolshevik immigrants from the
United States; on April 29 a bomb which had been sent to him
through the mail blew off his servant's hands. On the following
day the New York Post Office turned over to the police packages
similar to the one sent to Hardwick. They were addressed to
Attorney-General Palmer, Postmaster General Burleson, J. P.
Morgan, John D. Rockefeller, and other government officials
and capitalists. All the packages contained bombs and eventually the total number accounted for reached thirty-six. The list
of intended recipients was regarded as strong evidence that the
bombs had been sent by an alien radical.

It was in this atmosphere of foreign conspirators and bomb
plots that Winnipeg faced the general strike. It was an atmosphere tending towards hysteria, and one can understand the
haste and the vigour with which the employing class and the
neutral public organized to protect themselves against the strike.
While the strike committee was organizing and directing, the
elements opposed to the strike had also been extremely active.
As already seen, the committee of a hundred had been organized
in 1918 to meet the challenge of a general strike. The experience
then derived proved of great value in 1919. When the strike
appeared inevitable the committee of a hundred was revived
and broadened under the name of committee of a thousand or,
more popularly, the citizens' committee. This technique of
meeting the strike was repeated in the United States during the
great steel strike which lasted from September 22 to January 8,
1920; but the citizens' committees which were set up in the
various American steel towns[58] appear to have specialized in
man-handling labour leaders whereas the Winnipeg committee,
in its early stages at least, was chiefly concerned with the maintenance of those public services which the strike had partially
paralyzed. Headquarters of the citizens' committee was set up
in the barn-like Board of Trade building on Main Street,

[58]William Z. Foster, *The Great Steel Strike and Its Lessons*, New York, 1920,
pp. 177, 188-9.

on the site of the present Federal building, and the machinery for breaking the strike soon began to function smoothly.

The citizens' committee was composed mainly of members of the managerial class and professional men.   It was supported by wholesale and retail merchants, building contractors, managers of hotels and theatres, banking and insurance and other financial men, grain brokers, real estate salesmen, and professional men such as doctors, dentists, lawyers, and chartered accountants.

The nature of the support given to the citizens' committee is indicated by the elements composing the Winnipeg Citizens' League which was formed after the strike to organize support for anti-labour candidates in the civic elections.   The author has seen a list of prospects from whom the League anticipated financial assistance.   It included the following:

Wholesale Grocers Ass'n.	Provincial Exhibitors Ass'n.
Canadian Manufacturers Ass'n.	Western Canada Fire,
Bankers Ass'n.	Underwriters Ass'n.
Winnipeg Motor Trades Ass'n.	Winnipeg Life Underwriters Ass'n.
Manitoba Mortgage Loan Ass'n.	Winnipeg Dental Society.
Retail Merchants Ass'n.	Manitoba Law Society.
Winnipeg Grain Exchange.	Film Exchange Managers Ass'n.
Western Retail Lumbermen's Ass'n.	Manitoba Association of Architects.
Builders Exchange.	Real Estate Exchange.
Royal Alexandra Hotel.	Institute of Chartered
Fort Garry Hotel.	Accountants of Man.
Imperial Oil Co. Ltd.	Manitoba Medical Society.

The chairman of the citizens' committee was A. K. Godfrey, a grain and lumber merchant.   Other prominent members were Edward Parnell, manager of the Parnell Bread Company, J. E. Botterell, a grain broker, and Adams, a harness manufacturer.   Isaac Pitblado, A. J. Andrews, J. B. Coyne, T. Sweatman, E. K. Williams, and A. L. Crossin, all members of the Winnipeg Bar, were extremely active on the committee.[59] Associated with the business and professional groups were other "white collar workers."   Many of these were office workers who, in spite of low pay, identified themselves with the citizens' committee.

[59] *Manitoba Free Press*, Dec. 9, 1919, *The King* v. *R. B. Russell*, testimony of Mayor Gray.   Preliminary hearing, *The King* v. *William Ivens et al.*, testimony of Edward Parnell.

In general, the members of the citizens' committee regarded themselves as neutral in regard to the dispute in the metal and building trades which led to the strike. They claimed, however, that a general strike which paralyzed the necessary services of life in a modern city was everybody's concern. While refusing to discuss the merits of the original dispute they set out to end the general strike, claiming that the original dispute could be discussed later. "The Citizens' Committee," said Edward Parnell, "was gotten up for no other purpose but keeping law and order in the city and endeavouring to help run the public utilities and keep the city's affairs moving."[60] Through all the meetings of the committee, asserted Parnell, the merits and demerits of the labour question were never discussed by the members. "They took no part directly or indirectly in that matter, but simply tried to bring about a condition that would prevent bloodshed and keep the utilities going." J. E. Botterell, the grain broker, supported this claim. The object of the citizens' committee, he said, was to back up constituted authority and to do anything in its power to maintain the public utilities. "We did not take any part between employer and employee," he asserted.[61]

It may be noted that while the citizens' committee was theoretically neutral, in practice it was opposed to the strike committee. This was inevitable since the strike committee was charged with operating the strike and it was the strike which was causing the paralysis of the public utilities which the citizens' committee wished to terminate. Whatever the merits of the dispute, the ironmasters had not taken any open action to paralyze the city as the strike leaders had done.

From the beginning most of the members of the citizens' committee were firmly convinced that they were confronted with no ordinary strike but with an incipient revolution, directed in reality from Moscow. This is not surprising. In this year of the "big Red scare" every major strike in the United States and Canada was described as Bolshevist. Mayor Ole Hanson had described the Seattle general strike as "of itself the weapon

---

[60]*Ibid.*
[61]*Ibid.*, testimony of J. E. Botterell.

of revolution, all the more dangerous, because quiet."[62]   Similar
denunciations were levelled at all the other major strikes in the
United States and Canada in this period.[63]   The members of
the citizens' committee had read of the Seattle strike in February
and of the bomb outrages in April.   Nearer home they had
read the lurid utterances of radical labour leaders at the Calgary
convention.   They assumed that the Winnipeg strike was the
beginning of the revolution and they were thoroughly alarmed.
Because they belonged to classes in society which had little
intimate contact with labour, they assumed further that the
entire labour movement was composed of dangerous radicals,
most of them aliens, determined to wreck established institutions
of government and inaugurate a Bolshevist regime.   Whether
they were right or wrong in their assumption that the strike was
intended as a revolution is still a controversial point.   Yet
there can be no doubt about the genuine alarm of the members
of the committee or about their sincere and in many cases
unselfish devotion to the defence of the institutions which they
valued.

The alarm of the committee is obvious in the tone of the
Winnipeg Citizen, the paper which the committee began to
publish on May 19.   A representative utterance was the
Citizen's editorial of May 27: "No thoughtful citizen can any
longer doubt that the so-called general strike is in reality revolution—or a daring attempt to overthrow the present industrial
and governmental system."   The *Citizen* was supported in this
view by the *Free Press* in its bulletin of May 22.   Under the
lurid heading, "The Great Dream of the Winnipeg Soviet," the
Free Press argued:

"There is no doubt as to what was in the minds of [the strike leaders].
They had no intention of depriving the city entirely of food and milk,
light and power.   No, their intention was to take over—that is to
commandeer, which is the very essence of sovereignty—those neces-
sities of life and distribute them according to their pleasure, thus
making an invincible weapon of their possession of these essentials."

The story of the citizens' committee was one of progress
from comparatively mild measures at first to drastic efforts at

[62]Crook, *The General Strike, Labor's Tragic Weapon*, 534.
[63]See especially Hiller, *The Strike, A Study in Collective Action*, 175.

suppression of the strike in its closing stages. The committee began by organizing volunteers to man the public utilities; it ended by securing the use of special police and the arrest of the principal strike leaders. This evolution is typical of the effect of a prolonged strike upon the anti-strike party which eventually feels itself forced to extremes by the progress of events.

Early activities of the committee were concerned with the organization of volunteers and with the mobilization of opinion against the strike. The Board of Trade building, according to the committee, became the liveliest place in town.[64] From there the committee directed the fire brigade and other public utilities. Sub-committees were functioning in every room. Outside, the street was lined with cars and drivers ready to undertake any duty.

As a result of these activities the city put volunteers in the fire brigade, the electrical department, and the waterworks. The volunteers were chiefly white collar workers and had all the difficulties of amateurs attempting jobs which in many cases required experience and skill. When a storm tore off part of the roof of the Children's Hospital in June and left electric wiring dangerously exposed the "volunteer metal workers" who came from the citizens' committee were unable to repair it and additional assistance had to be secured. However, considering the difficulties, the volunteers were reasonably successful. Water pressure was raised to normal, to the intense gratification of people who lived above the second storey. Later, when volunteers were called for to staff the postal services, the citizens' committee helped to provide the volunteers.[65]

The task of rallying opinion against the strike required the publication of a newspaper after the *Free Press* and the *Tribune* and the *Telegram* had been forced to shut down on May 16. The citizens' committee accordingly began publication of the *Winnipeg Citizen* on May 19. Its first number contained a statement by the citizens' committee: "Among the objects of this committee may be mentioned the maintenance of law and order, the carrying on of the essential services necessary to

[64]*Winnipeg Citizen*, May 20, 1919.
[65]Preliminary hearing, *The King* v. *William Ivens et al.*, testimony of Mayor Gray and J. K. Sparling.

preserve the lives and health of the whole community, including the strikers, but more particularly, the little children, invalid soldiers and the sick." The principal object of the *Citizen* was political. Just how thoroughly it castigated the strikers is indicated by a list of headings from the issue of May 20:

The Opportunity Lost by Labour Through Bad Leadership
The Gagging of the Press
A Mis-statement Nailed
Trying to Close Restaurants
"We are Running the City"
The Alien Connection?
Who is Running the City?

Once the city newspapers were able to resume publication they strongly supported the citizens' committee. The *Free Press* under the vigorous and hard-hitting direction of its editor, J. W. Dafoe, was particularly overwhelming in its criticism of the strike committee. Dafoe, a great Liberal and at this time heart and soul behind the Progressive movement, was not sympathetic to labour. In his personal correspondence, he usually referred to Winnipeg labour leaders as "the Reds." The other two newspapers, the *Tribune* and the *Telegram*, were especially clear in their condemnation of the strikers, although their editorials were not couched in Dafoe's thunderous style. The stand taken by Dafoe was later defended by his successor as editor of the *Free Press*, George V. Ferguson:

He [Dafoe] was more friendlily disposed to the cause of labour than most labour people in Winnipeg believed. But he refused to countenance a strike which struck at the state. He considered the performance an outrage against society. . . . The police and the postal workers had joined the strikers. This, in Dafoe's view, was indefensible and for years he opposed the efforts to reinstate the men dismissed at that time. Society as a whole, he believed, had certain general rights which were indefeasible. No warring factions within that society, factions composed of trade unions and employers' associations, had the right to harm the whole. When that happened he was against all of them.[66]

The activities and publications of the citizens' committee were not, of course, accepted by the strikers without protest.

[66]George V. Ferguson, *John W. Dafoe*, Toronto, 1948, 25-6.

"Under the innocuous title of '*The Winnipeg Citizen*'," snorted the *Western Labor News* of May 21, "a terrorist paper has been published in this city. While proclaiming itself to be neither for nor against the strikers, it proceeds to paint the strike 'Red'." On May 23 the *News* quoted the manager of a large city plant who was alleged to have said, "What we should do is to line a few of these boneheads up against a wall and shoot them—I only wish they would start something." On May 28 the *News* continued to castigate the *Citizen*, this time alleging "Gross and Despicable Misrepresentations."

So the controversy went on. Each paper was bitter in its condemnation of the other. Each catered to its own public, which heard only one side of the question.

While opinion in many quarters of Winnipeg was hardening against the strikers, a similar development took place in the rural areas of the West. The farmer had never had much knowledge of or sympathy with the labour movement. The agrarian movement, which was soon to sweep farmer governments into power in Ontario, Alberta, and Manitoba, and to give the Progressives sixty-six federal seats, was already well under way. Yet the movement did not make the farmer any more sympathetic to labour.[67] Several reasons for the breach may be indicated. The conflict of interest between farmer and urban worker, in an economy in which industry was protected and agriculture was not, was particularly sharp in a period of advanced inflation in which labour was regarded by the farmers as more successful in protecting its interests.[68] Equally important was the conflict of political philosophies. Neither in theory nor in practice did the Progressives contemplate extensive socialist reforms. In practice they undertook to secure such objectives as tariff revision and reduction of freight rates. These reforms were calculated to secure a re-allocation of the national income in favour of the farmer, and could, of course, be achieved within the existing framework of political and economic institutions. The Progressive movement stemmed

[67]Such co-operation as there was in the Progressive movement between farmers and urban labour was verbal and merely local and determined by the character of certain constituencies; but the co-operation was not extensive. (W. L. Morton, *The Progressive Party in Canada*, Toronto, 1950, pp. 117-18.)

[68]*Ibid.*

from two opposing theories but neither had much in common with socialism. T. A. Crerar, the exponent of one theory, envisaged the Progressives as a party composed of the representatives of all classes but dominated by or at least strongly influenced by the farmers. Such a party would secure those objectives which the farmer desired. Henry Wise Wood, the great Alberta agrarian philosopher, differed with Crerar and maintained that the party should consist only of farmers. While accepting the view of a class struggle, he believed the struggle between classes would find its reconciliation not in revolution and the classless society but in an equilibrium of conflicting interests.[69] Acceptance of the philosophy and programme of the Progressives increased the distaste of the farmers for the Marxism frequently expounded by labour radicals; moreover, extremists like Russell and Johns were often regarded as representative of the whole labour movement.

In Manitoba, the congenital antipathy of the farmers was increased when the strike cut off Winnipeg for a time as a consuming area for milk, live-stock and other produce. The trade in wheat was also disrupted. Even the rural telephone service in many areas was shut off by the strike.

As a result farmer opinion seems to have been unanimous against the strike and practically every rural newspaper in the province condemned it. A representative list of quotations will illustrate this attitude.

The Age, Gladstone, May 29: Incensed by the arrogant and intolerant attitude of the strike committee the citizens finally took matters into their own hands and organized to carry on the necessary public utilities.

The Boissevain *Recorder*, May 22: Unions are all alright providing they act reasonable but it looks now as if labor is so strongly organized that they propose riding roughshod over principles.

The *Empire-Advance*, Virden, May 27: Union is alright when rightly [directed], but in the present case so-called union is all wrong, because of a large measure of indifference, on the part of the members generally of the various unions who have permitted the wrong leaders to assume places of prominence.

[69]*Ibid.* L. A. Wood, *A History of Farmers' Movements in Canada*, Toronto, 1924, p. 100.

So it went on. Expressions of opinion from the rural press varied but the general attitude was the same. The Birtle *Eye-Witness* warned on May 20 that, "Protraction of present conditions may force [the] general public to take measures for self-protection." The Manitou *Western Canadian* playfully suggested on May 29 the dire consequences if the farmers struck. Even the Neepawa *Register* which had appeared favourable to the strike on May 22, had swung into line by May 29 and was approving the action of the dominion government in upholding "constitutional authority in Canada."

The labour leaders never gave any indication of realizing the importance of capturing rural support. Here was a workers' movement in a community predominantly rural. To succeed it must avoid antagonizing the rural population. A benevolent provincial government, reflecting rural opinion sympathetic to the strike, would have very much strengthened the hands of the strike leaders. In the Homestead strike in Illinois in 1894 the sympathetic attitude of Governor Altgeld very much strengthened the strikers until the intervention of the federal government.[70] The Norris administration, although officially Liberal, was just as much a farmers' government as the Progressive government of John Bracken which succeeded it in 1922. Any evidence of sympathy for the strikers would have been communicated to the government by rural M.L.A.'s. There was no such evidence, and the strike leaders, like previous western labour leaders, made little or no effort to capture rural support. On the other hand, the R.N.W.M.P. and the citizens' committee undertook to align the farmers against the strike. Commissioner Perry appeared before the executive of the Saskatchewan Grain Growers' Association on May 21 and denounced the O.B.U. as a revolutionary organization seeking the confiscation of private property and the establishment of a Communist form of government.[71] On June 5 a representative of the Winnipeg citizens' committee assured the executive that there was actual revolution in Winnipeg and appealed for the

[70]Matthew Josephson, *The Politicos 1865-1896*, New York, 1938, pp. 573-5.

[71]*Minutes of the Executive of the Saskatchewan Grain Growers' Association*, May 21, 1919, p. 111. I am indebted for this citation to Professor W. L. Morton of the University of Manitoba.

support of agriculture.   The result was the passing of a resolution which viewed with concern the industrial unrest in the
dominion and which expressed opposition to any attempt to
overthrow constituted authority.[72]   It is unlikely that the
Winnipeg labour leaders would have received much rural
support even if they had tried.   J. S. Woodsworth later addressed
the executive of the Saskatchewan Grain Growers' Association
and asserted that the Winnipeg strike had not been a revolution;
but the ensuing discussion indicated that many members were
not much influenced by his argument.[73]   In view of the initial
antipathy to be overcome, efforts before or during the strike to
win rural support, had they been made, would probably have
been unsuccessful.   However, no such efforts were made.

The strike committee was brought into contact with three
governments: municipal, provincial, and dominion.   Each was
concerned with two problems: to negotiate a settlement and,
in the meantime, to preserve the essential services in Winnipeg.
These governments, of course, were not equally active in their
efforts to secure these objectives.

The strike committee was, of necessity, in constant touch
with the City Council which at first, through the Mayor,
endeavoured to secure a settlement.   The Council was also
concerned, from the beginning, with the maintenance of public
utilities and had sponsored the negotiations which had led to
the resumption of milk and bread deliveries.   The Council too
had accepted aid from the citizens' committee in manning the
fire brigade and the water works.

The Council was, of course, divided.   Aldermen Queen and
Heaps were closely associated with the strike and always
championed the strikers.   The remaining members, including
Mayor Gray, were more or less on the other side.   This led to
some vigorous clashes and particularly a peppery argument
between the Mayor and Queen.   At a session of the food committee, of which Queen was chairman, the Mayor, a member
ex officio, attempted to speak and made some reference to
constituted authority.   Queen who regarded him as obstructive,
lost his temper and shouted that he didn't want to hear about

[72]*Ibid.*, June 5, 1919, pp. 53-4.
[73]*Ibid.*, Sept. 19, 1919, p. 56.

constituted authority, a remark which told against him at his
trial.[74]

The Mayor's early efforts at settlement produced little but
mutual recrimination. He made overtures to both parties
early in the strike. According to his testimony at the preliminary strike trial, he conferred with the ironmasters of the
three companies concerned, on May 19 or 20 and again on
May 21. The conferences elicited only the information that
the ironmasters considered that negotiations in the metal trades
dispute were not advisable until the general strike was ended.
Gray had asked Russell for a written statement "to the effect
that a recognition of the Metal Trades Council would open up
the possibilities of reaching a settlement."[75] The central strike
committee, having been informed of this proposal on May 19,
indicated that it would favour a settlement "just as soon as ALL
employers agree to recognize organized labor and negotiate
schedules." The matter was referred to a special sub-committee
and there, for the time being, it rested.

The next effort at a settlement came from a letter sent to
Mayor Gray by H. E. Barker, chairman of the committee of
train service employees, offering his services as a mediator.[76]
This led to a midnight meeting called by Mayor Gray. It was
attended by the Mayor, Aldermen Fisher and Simpson, Messrs.
Winning and Russell of the strike committee, Andrews and
Sweatman, acting as individuals (presumably representing the
citizens' committee), Carroll and English of the running trades,
D. J. Scott and R. B. Graham, Crown Prosecutor for the eastern
judicial district. This meeting probably occurred on May 25-26
since it was reported in the *Western Labor News* of May 26. It
was abortive and led mainly to a sharp exchange between
A. J. Andrews, who insisted that the general strike must end
before negotiations began, and R. B. Russell, who repudiated
this idea.[77]

The breakdown of this conference was followed by a different
approach to the strike on the part of the City Council. At a

[74]Preliminary hearing, *The King* v. *William Ivens et al.*, testimony of Mayor Gray.
[75]*Western Labor News*, May 20, 1919.
[76]Preliminary hearing, *The King* v. *William Ivens et al.*, testimony of Mayor Gray.
[77]*Ibid.*, testimony of R. B. Graham. *Western Labor News*, May 26, 1919.

Council meeting of May 26 Aldermen Sparling and F. O. Fowler led a frontal attack against the striking firemen.   As the policy which they proposed was later applied to the other public services and especially to the police, it should be carefully noted.[78]

The Sparling-Fowler motion proposed: (*a*) that no union should exist among the Winnipeg firemen which was in affiliation with any organization "whose orders or commands it may be subject to obey"; (*b*) that the supreme governing power of the fire brigade be vested in the Council; and (*c*) that every one applying for a position on the fire brigade sign an application promising never to strike until a dispute between a firemen's union and the city had been arbitrated.   Finally, and most significantly, the applicant was to promise never to participate in a sympathetic strike.

This resolution challenged the whole position of the striking firemen in relation to the general strike.   It produced a sharp dispute in the Council.   Nor was this all.   A second resolution sponsored by Alderman Fulford was introduced calling for the dismissal of all employees in the civic services who had struck on May 15.   Both resolutions passed by a vote of nine to five. Queen and Heaps were supported by Aldermen Robinson, Simpson and Wiginton, but the rest of the Council voted against them.   Thus was the gauntlet flung down to the striking civic employees.

Extension of the Sparling-Fowler policy followed immediately.   On May 29 Mayor Gray informed the Council that the police were being asked to sign an agreement similar to that required of the firemen.[79]   This was the move which led to the dismissal of the police force and to the subsequent disorders.

The provincial government of Premier T. C. Norris, a Liberal administration with a fine record of reform,[80] was not so directly concerned as the City Council with the maintenance of the civic services except the telephone system which was owned and operated by the province.   As the leader of what was

[78]*Ibid.*, May 28, 1919.

[79]*Ibid.*, May 30, 1919.

[80]The Norris administration had passed legislation providing for amendment of the electoral laws, reform of the civil service, direct legislation (later declared *ultra vires*), prohibition, rural credits, workmen's compensation, mothers' allowances and child welfare.

in effect a farmers' government, Norris was not particularly favourable to labour. Yet he made several efforts to settle the strike and, at the end of May, was attempting to secure agreement between the ironmasters and the strike committee over the principle of collective bargaining.[81] He discovered, as had Gray, that no agreement was possible. "We have felt that the general sympathetic strike situation should be cleared up before our own matters should be dealt with," wrote the metal masters to the premier on May 28.[82] This was an attitude widely held among the non-labour elements in Winnipeg. As the strike committee was equally insistent that concessions must precede the ending of the general strike, negotiations were bound to fail.

The dominion government concerned itself with the maintenance of law and order in Winnipeg almost from the beginning of the strike. No dominion government could have ignored so serious a catastrophe as the Winnipeg strike. The Union Government, under the leadership of Sir Robert Borden, was particularly anxious, in view of its waning prestige, to avoid the discredit of a breakdown of law and order. Shortly after the armistice on November 11, 1918, the government had begun to disintegrate. Confronted by a hostile Quebec, by a West which became increasingly restive under a continued protectionism, and by demands within the ranks for a return to straight Conservative rule, the Union Government by May 1919 was a doomed administration.[83] Even in its palmy days the government had never been especially *persona grata* with labour as a whole, although strong labour support had been anticipated after the appointment of a former vice-president of the Telegraphers' Union, Hon. Gideon Robertson, as minister of labour; the appointment of Robertson, a conservative trade unionist, had pleased the labour right wing but had alienated the left. Occupying a precarious position in its relation to the country as a whole and to labour in particular, the government was certain to take vigorous measures to terminate the strike. This

[81]*Western Labor News*, May 30, 1919.
[82]*Ibid.*
[83]A former Conservative minister, Hon. Robert Rogers, demanded a return to straight Conservative rule, a view which was endorsed in Toronto by the Central Conservative Association and in Winnipeg by a Conservative provincial convention. *Cambridge History of the British Empire*, VI, 758.

was rendered doubly certain by the fact that the minister of justice, who soon became involved in the strike, was Hon. Arthur Meighen, an able and determined man. In addition to considerations of general prestige, the administration was affected by the strike of post-office employees who were civil servants of the dominion government.

The general policy of the dominion government was announced by Sir Robert Borden in the House of Commons on May 27 and consistently followed to the end of the strike.[84]

In dealing with the situation at Winnipeg there are certain fundamental considerations to which this Government is committed. . . . In the first place, we are absolutely determined that law and order should be maintained, and in the second place, we are of opinion that members of the Civil Service cannot be permitted to disregard their public duties and to dislocate the public service under the conditions which have arisen in the city of Winnipeg.

Borden then pledged his government to maintain law and order and to discountenance the strike of postal employees. The application of this policy fell largely to Borden's colleagues: Robertson, Meighen, and Major-General Mewburn, the minister of militia.

Robertson was already in Winnipeg before Borden's announcement of May 27. His first objective was to break the postal strike. He instructed the Winnipeg postmaster to announce that all employees must return to work by May 26; failing to do so they were to regard themselves as discharged. This declaration placed the postal employees in a serious dilemma, a clear example of the difficulty of preserving neutrality during a period of civil disturbance. Were the employees to obey their employers or continue in support of the Trades and Labor Council? In order to persuade them to return McIntyre, the postmaster, held a meeting on May 25 which Robertson addressed. The turnout of striking employees was not large, however, and on May 26 only between 75 and 100, out of 400 strikers, resumed work. McIntyre then began to take on new employees.[85]

[84]*House of Commons Debates*, 1919, p. 2853.
[85]Preliminary hearing, *The King* v. *William Ivens et al.*, testimony of P. C. McIntyre.

To guarantee the maintenance of order in Winnipeg the government took steps to ensure the presence of adequate military and police forces. The nature of these preparations was later revealed by Hon. Peter Heenan in the House of Commons in 1926 after he had had access to the files of the departments concerned.[86] The various steps in the government's policy of preparedness may be briefly traced. On May 14, General Ketchen, the commanding officer in Winnipeg, advised the military council at Ottawa that Mayor Gray had communicated to him the intention of calling upon the military to protect property.[87] On May 15 instructions were issued that a squadron of the R.N.W.M.P. returning from overseas should be demobilized at Winnipeg and placed at the disposal of Commissioner Perry. On May 19 Ketchen wired Ottawa that he had called out a percentage of the active militia. On May 23 Brigadier-General F. W. Hill was ordered to go to Montreal to meet the 27th Battalion who were *en route* to Winnipeg from overseas. He was instructed to ascertain whether the whole or a part of the battalion would remain on duty during the period of emergency in Winnipeg. He was also advised that at Montreal eight Lewis guns were to be placed on board the train carrying the 27th and another twelve at Smith's Falls. These guns were to be packed in ordinary packing boxes and labelled regimental baggage, 27th Battalion.

The state of military preparedness in Winnipeg was indicated by Major-General Mewburn who announced in the House of Commons on May 23 that the four militia units (90th Regiment, 79th Regiment, Fort Garry Horse, and 13th Battery) were completely filled up with volunteers and that there were plenty of reserves available in case of trouble.[88] On May 26 General Ketchen reported the safe arrival in Winnipeg of the machine guns. The 27th Battalion which also arrived by the same train was promptly disbanded. A member of the battalion told the writer that only two members had volunteered for service in Winnipeg. Even without the 27th, Robertson was able to wire the Cabinet council on May 27 that Ketchens' arrangements were adequate and admirable.

---

[86]*House of Commons Debates*, 1926, pp. 4004-4005.
[87]For Gray's attitude toward the strike see p. 84.
[88]*House of Commons Debates*, 1919, p. 2753.

Robertson was opposed to any undue conciliation in the early stages of the strike.   He felt that a concession over the issue of collective bargaining would be interpreted by the strikers as a victory and, what was worse, as a vindication of the sympathetic strike.   This is shown by his telegram to the Cabinet on May 25: "This is not an opportune time to make a declaration in favour of principle of collective bargaining as it would be grasped as an excuse by strikers to claim they have forced the government and thereby proved success of sympathetic strike."   Robertson predicted that either the strike would shortly be called off "or a last desperate move made to make it successful."   In either case he could see no advantage in a concession on the issue of collective bargaining.

The great stumbling block to all negotiations was the sympathetic strike.   None of the parties to the dispute would have disagreed with the dramatized explanation by the *Western Labor News* on May 29, although they would have differed over the allocation of praise and blame among the various parties.

The playlet was entitled "A Fine Chorus" and read:

Senator Robertson:—I can do nothing till the posties return to work.

Premier Norris:—I can do nothing till you call off the sympathetic strike.

City Council:—We can do nothing till the civic employees return.

Board of Trade:—We can do nothing till you all go back.

The Strikers:—(Discordant Voice) We can do nothing till you all come forward.

There were a number of indications in Winnipeg during the closing days of May that the general position, from the viewpoint of opponents of the strike, had improved.   Most of the gasoline filling stations had reopened by May 22, according to the *Free Press*.   On the same day, May 22, the *Free Press*, which had set up a wireless station on the roof of its building, established communications with the outside world.   A message was sent to the University of North Dakota, near Grand Forks, for general transmission.

Winnipeg, May 22, 1919.

By Winnipeg Free Press Wireless:

First uncensored despatch filed from Winnipeg by a newspaper since joining up of general strike by telegraphers, noon May 17th.

All reports of violence in Winnipeg unfounded; but postal service utterly demoralized. . . .

Abundance of food. Bread and milk deliveries maintained. Water, light, gas services operating.

General strike being continued including stoppage of street cars and suspension of newspapers.[89]

By May 24 the three newspapers had resumed publication. The Winnipeg *Telegram* celebrated this event with an editorial, facetiously headed, "Once More, Good Evening!" The post office began taking on new workers as soon as the expiration on May 26 of the period set in its ultimatum to its old employees. The *Free Press* on May 27 announced a rush for the position of postal clerks. By May 30 the postmaster reported a total staff of over three hundred and mail deliveries had been resumed in the more congested areas of the city.[90] According to the *Free Press* of May 30 the ultimatum of the city council had resulted in repudiation of the strike by a large percentage of civic workers. The City Hall, said the *Free Press*, was crowded all day of Thursday, May 29, with office help anxious to sign the anti-strike pledge. On the other hand the central committee on May 26 had decided to call out the railway conductors and the engineers.[91] Nevertheless, even allowing for variations in the interpretation of news, there appeared to be some basis for the *Free Press* heading on May 29, "Strike Situation Greatly Improved During Past Week."

However, while the effects of the strike had been modified in Winnipeg, there had been an epidemic of strikes in many other Canadian cities. Whether these were "sympathetic" strikes was later a matter of some controversy. The Winnipeg strike leaders later claimed they were the result of local grievances. To a considerable extent this was true. Yet the coincidence of strikes all over the country at this time appears to indicate that the Winnipeg strike had imparted some impetus to the strike movement in various other centres.

[89]*Manitoba Free Press*, May 23, 1919. [Set up on May 23 but published as part of a general issue on June 4.]

[90]*Ibid.*, May 31, 1919.

[91]*Western Labor News*, May 28, 1919.

The result fell far short of the general tie-up which some of the strike leaders kept predicting; but there were sporadic strikes in a number of places. The superintendent of the western division of the Dominion Express Company later testified that there had been strikes among the expressmen at Calgary, Edmonton, Lethbridge, and Medicine Hat.[92]   In Calgary the street cars ceased to run and the hotels and restaurants closed.[93] Production of coal in the Drumheller area was interrupted by a strike of the miners on May 24. According to the mine owners, S. M. McMullen and Samuel Drumheller, the strike was organized by a man named J. O'Sullivan, whose relations with the mine owners had not been amicable since he was regarded as a dangerous revolutionary.[94]

The most formidable challenge of labour, during this period, outside Winnipeg, came from Toronto.   There, as in Winnipeg, a dispute developed in the metal trades in which workers demanded an 8-hour day and a 44-hour week. This led to a strike vote, sponsored by the Toronto Trades and Labor Council, in which delegates allegedly representing 10,000 employees voted for a general strike, with delegates representing about 2,000 opposing it. According to the *Mail and Empire*, a third group of delegates representing about 8,000 members did not vote.[95]   At 2 A.M. on May 27 a vote was carried to put the matter into the hands of a committee of fifteen. The committee was given power to call a strike at 10 A.M. on May 28 of such unions as it considered necessary to support the metal workers.

The strike was temporarily postponed owing to the proposal of negotiations sponsored by the dominion government. A delegation of twenty-four left Toronto for Ottawa on the evening of May 28.   It included representatives of the City Council, the Metal Trades Council, the Employers' Association and the District Labor Council.   This assortment, said the *Mail and Empire* optimistically, "all travelled in a special Pullman,

---

[92]Preliminary hearing, *The King* v. *William Ivens et al.*, testimony of William M. Gordon.

[93]Crook, *The General Strike, Labor's Tragic Weapon*, 550.

[94]*Manitoba Free Press*, Dec. 6, 1919, *The King* v. *R. B. Russell*, testimony of S. M. McMullen and Samuel Drumheller; Dec. 10, 1919, testimony of James Gough.

[95]*Mail and Empire*, Toronto, May 27, 1919.

which provided a great opportunity for them to discuss matters during the Journey.''[96] Juxta-position did not produce agreement either on the way to Ottawa or in the day-long conference which was held there on May 29. The employers made a proposal at 7 P.M. that the dispute over the 44-hour week should be arbitrated. This offer was wired to Toronto and there rejected, according to the *Mail and Empire*, by the strike committee and the Metal Trades Council.[97] The general strike was accordingly called on Friday, May 30. The strike fell far short of being "general." The *Mail and Empire* on May 31 estimated that 8,000 workmen were out, while W. H. Crook, author of a standard work, *The General Strike, Labor's Tragic Weapon*, who is pro-labour in sympathy, estimates 15,000.[98] However, there was always a possibility of the strike spreading. The anti-strike elements in Toronto were alarmed and, in true Toronto style, organized a committee of *ten thousand* to function as did the citizens' committee of Winnipeg. Meanwhile, as will be seen in the next chapter, a situation was developing in Vancouver which was to end in a much more serious and more general strike than the one in Toronto.

By the end of May the lines of battle were clearly drawn in Winnipeg. The strikers had organized the machinery to conduct and maintain the strike. The forces of labour had been mobilized and held in line with remarkable efficiency. There had been some defections, in the postal service for instance, but most of the strikers of May 15 were still out on May 30. The strike committee had adjusted its policy to the need for maintaining some of the public services, at least on a partial basis. It had kept its men off the streets and out of trouble to an amazing degree.

The citizens' committee on the other hand had organized the anti-strike forces with equal skill. The force of volunteers who had helped to staff the fire brigade, the waterworks, the post office and so forth had accomplished much in modifying the early impact of the strike.

[96]*Ibid.*, May 29, 1919.

[97]*Ibid.*, May 30, 1919. *House of Commons Debates*, 1919, p. 2953, statement by Sir Robert Borden.

[98]Crook, *The General Strike, Labor's Tragic Weapon*, 552.

Negotiations during the period had been fairly continuous but abortive.   In view of the organization of the contending parties and their complete inability to understand each other, the prospects of an early solution seemed dim.   The train of developments which broke the strike had not yet begun on May 30.

CHAPTER THREE

The Strike: Last Phase

I T W A S the morning of Saturday, June 21. A stormy meeting was in progress in a room in the red-brick Royal Alexandra Hotel.[1] Presiding over it was Gideon Robertson, the minister of labour, who had just arrived in Winnipeg to end the strike. With him were Commissioner Perry in the khaki uniform of an officer of the R.N.W.M.P.; A. J. Andrews, who had been acting as legal representative of the department of justice; Mayor Gray, looking haggard and worried; Anderson, a machinist and member of the strike committee; and three determined-looking soldier-strikers, Martin, Farnell, and Dunn.

Robertson by his dramatic intervention had ended the Winnipeg strike of May 1918, but it was a very different situation which he now encountered. The strike was approaching its crisis and the atmosphere had become infinitely more tense than at the end of May. On June 4 the strike committee had again suspended deliveries of bread, milk, and ice. The police had been dismissed on June 9, and the appearance of special police on the streets on June 10 had been accompanied by some disorder. Most alarming had been the intervention of the soldiers. Impatient of inactivity, the ex-soldiers supporting the strike had begun a series of parades on May 31; this had been answered by similar parades of the anti-strike returned soldiers. Assembling of large crowds in the streets had created a situation in which disorders might break out at any time.

[1]Preliminary hearing, *The King* v. *William Ivens et al.*, testimony of Mayor Gray. *Western Labor News*, June 23, 1919. *House of Commons Debates*, 1919, p. 3844, announcement by N. W. Rowell.

Mayor Gray had tried to check the parades by the issuance of proclamations on June 5 and June 11, and for a time they had stopped. Yet the situation had become increasingly tense. Even the elements had added to the conflict on the evening of June 14 when Winnipeg was struck by a violent storm of rain and wind which did a great deal of damage, ripping off part of the roof of the Children's Hospital. Only the night before Robertson's council of war, a noisy meeting had been held in front of the City Hall and soldier speakers had boldly declared that they would organize a silent parade in support of the strikers on the following day. To prevent this catastrophe, Robertson had summoned the meeting in his hotel suite.

The Mayor was speaking now, looking very much the tired liberal. In the early stages of the strike he had made a sincere effort at conciliation. This had brought criticism from both sides. The strikers had called him a tool of reaction; members of the citizens' committee had considered him a spineless accepter of revolution. Gradually he had become exasperated with what he regarded as the obstinacy of the strike leaders, and the parades had completed his conversion to the viewpoint of the citizens' committee.

Now he was attempting to dissuade the soldiers. There must be no parade that day he said. Parades were in open defiance of his proclamations of June 5 and June 11. Only this morning he had issued another proclamation to the same effect. There must be no parade, the Mayor reiterated. If there was one he would not be responsible for the consequence. Outside on Main Street the crowds were already gathering and the soldiers remained defiant. Would the Mayor withdraw the street-cars which had just reappeared on the streets?

No, the Mayor would not.

Then, said the soldiers, they would hold the parade at whatever cost.

There was a tense silence. Somebody suggested that the soldiers might be satisfied with a meeting in the Industrial Bureau. Mr. Andrews offered to try to secure it, but no agreement was reached.

The telephone rang. Robertson answered and said it was for Gray. Gray listened and looked even more haggard. It was Newton, the acting chief of police. Crowds were rapidly gathering between the City Hall and Portage Avenue. Would the Mayor go to the City Hall?

The Mayor rose to leave. At the door he turned to warn the soldiers. The parade would be stopped, he flung out; by peaceful methods if possible, he added grimly, but if necessary by sterner measures.

He hurried to reach the City Hall. It was 1.45 P.M.

The crowd in front of the City Hall became more and more dense.[2] There were soldiers in uniform and civilians in working clothes or holiday attire. Some had come to parade and others to see the excitement. People were moving up and down Main Street in large groups. Soldiers had begun to line up the silent parade in the square. A. W. Puttee crossed the square, saw the crowds, and decided—wise man—that it would be healthier to go on a picnic down the river.

Gray hurried toward the City Hall by the back streets. He reached his office and telephoned Newton at the Rupert Street police station. The crowds continued to gather. Newton rang up again and urged Gray to call in the R.N.W.M.P. Desperate, the Mayor rushed to the barracks. There, in the presence of the provincial attorney-general, he asked Commissioner Perry to despatch his men to patrol the streets.

Before long the Mounties, immaculate in red or khaki coats, clattered along Portage and wheeled down Main. Armed with baseball bats they galloped into the crowd. Soon they were slowed to a walk in the seething mass of people, but still they pressed on, vigorously flailing out with their bats. They passed the City Hall, turned south and fought their way towards Portage amid a shower of tin cans, stones, bricks, and lumps of concrete. At length they reached McDermot Avenue, a sadly dishevelled group. Two of the horses were riderless.

Amid wild confusion the Mayor emerged on the front platform of the City Hall and read the Riot Act. His voice was

[2]The account of the "riot" of June 21 is based on the following: *Manitoba Free Press*, June 23, 1919; *Winnipeg Evening Tribune*, June 23, 1919; *Western Labor News*, June 23, 1919. Preliminary hearing, *The King* v. *William Ivens et al.*, testimony of Mayor Gray, A. C. McLaughlin, Captain Dunwoody. *Winnipeg Evening Tribune*, Feb. 16, 1920, *The King* v. *William Ivens et al.*, testimony of Corporal Campbell; *ibid.*, Feb. 20, 1920, testimony of Sergeant-Major Binning.

drowned in bedlam.   Again the Mounties came north and, as they did so, each transferred his club to the left hand and drew "an ugly-looking black revolver."   They swung left on William Avenue and fired a volley into the crowd.   They rounded the City Hall and slowed to a walk at the corner of Market and Main Streets.   Again they drove into the crowd which was surging around a street-car beleaguered and on fire in front of the City Hall.   This the crowd was attempting to upset.   The Mounties fired their second volley and Mike Sokolowiski, who stood in front of the Manitoba Hotel, was shot in the heart and killed instantly.   Other prostrate figures lay on the street and road.   The Mounties continued southward. Opposite the Confederation Life Building they encountered another shower of missiles and fired a third volley.   They reached McDermot Avenue and stopped for a few minutes to re-form.

As in many disturbances of this sort the question of who fired the first shot was later in dispute.   Gray testified that he had heard shots when the Mounties fought their way through the crowd the first time.   He claimed that they came from a direction which indicated that they could not have been fired by the police.   Several R.N.W.M.P. officers testified that there had been shots some time before the police had opened fire. Corporal Campbell reported that later he picked up several cartridges of .22 calibre in the Market Square whereas the police used .45's.   The *Western Labor News*, on the other hand, claimed that the police fired without any previous shooting having occurred.

The Mounties had now broken the opposition.   The rest was anti-climax.   Again they galloped north, this time with revolvers in holsters.   The crowd fled down side streets.   At the corner of Main and Market they were met by several companies of specials on foot who had issued from the Rupert Street police station.   The specials were in civilian attire with white armbands.   Many of them carried batons. Some, judging by their clothes, were farmers.   They had been mobilized in the station since 10 A.M.   They came out in waves led by a detachment under a Captain Dunwoody.   Now began the mopping-up operation. The specials formed lines at intervals of a block and swept Main Street clear of unauthorized persons.

At this time occurred the fight in Hell's Alley, one of the bitterest conflicts of the day. A portion of the crowd, estimated about two hundred, had taken refuge in the alley which ran between Market and James Streets. Here they were caught by specials who entered from both ends. The specials attacked with batons, and at one stage with revolvers, while the crowd retaliated with bricks and missiles. The struggle lasted only ten minutes, from 3.40 to 3.50, but produced twenty-seven casualties before the crowd was overwhelmed.

Meanwhile, after reading the Riot Act, just before the Mounties fired, Mayor Gray had driven to Osborne Barracks where he formally requested General Ketchen to aid the civic power to quell the disturbance. Order had been pretty well restored before the arrival of the military at Portage and Main. Cars bearing soldiers with fixed bayonets, and trucks carrying machine guns, drove up and down Main Street without challenge. The Mayor drove north as far as Redwood Avenue, urging the crowd to disperse. In Gray's office Dr. J. H. Leeming, the city bacteriologist, administered first aid to casualties before the transfer to hospital.

The riot area, now clear, was surrounded by a cordon of specials, Mounties, and soldiers. Main, and the streets for a block on either side, were guarded from the C.P.R. subway to the Board of Trade Building, and Portage to a point west of the Post Office. Soldiers patrolled the area. These consisted of the 90th Winnipeg Rifles, the 100th Winnipeg Grenadiers, the 106th Light Infantry, and the 79th Cameron Highlanders.

At 11 P.M. troops and police were withdrawn from the streets. The "riot" of June 21 was over.

The disorders of June 21 fulfilled the worst fears of the strike committee and demonstrated the wisdom of its policy of keeping the strikers off the streets. Even as late as the end of May no disturbances and very little activity on the streets had occurred. Then had begun the train of events which culminated in exactly the catastrophe which the strike committee had tried to avoid.

As late as June 6 the *Western Labor News* had been urging:

> Strikers, Hold your Horses!
> This is the hour when you can win
> Steady, Boys, Steady
> Keep quiet
> Do nothing
> Keep out of Trouble.

Already, however, the strike had entered upon the downward path which led to destruction.

It was the returned soldiers who made impossible the policy of passive resistance. For several years many had been living a life of action and excitement. They were home now, but not yet adjusted to a place in civilian life. Many of them felt strongly about the strike on one side or the other and they simply could not sit down and do nothing, passively awaiting the course of events. The soldiers had already shown their potential strength in the disorders of January and now at the end of May they made it felt even more vigorously. Their means of protest was the "peaceful parade" which was designed to be a harmless but significant warning to the authorities. Under some circumstances parades no doubt are of value in working off frustrated emotions. In the situation which prevailed in Winnipeg they were most dangerous. They began peacefully but ended in violence.

The first parade had occurred on the morning of Saturday, May 31, when a large number of soldiers and others swung down Kennedy Street to the legislative building.[3] They swarmed into the legislative chambers, where they presented to Premier Norris a demand that the principle of collective bargaining be recognized by the Government. Outside a large crowd shuffled impatiently, awaiting news. Norris courageously addressed the soldiers, amid boos and cat-calls, demanding that the sympathetic strike be called off. Afterwards he would attempt conciliation. Grumbling, the soldiers filed out. They stood around in uncertain groups in the rain. Someone shouted the suggestion that they go to the City Hall. Quickly the line formed again and the column swung northward. The city council was in

[3] *Western Labor News*, June 2, 1919.

earnest conclave, wrestling with the many problems created by the strike, when large numbers of soldiers began to clamber into the gallery. The meeting continued briefly while the Mayor apprehensively eyed the ever increasing crowd, and feared the gallery might collapse. Hastily he adjourned the meeting and pushed his way to the front steps to address the throng.[4] Like Norris he denounced the strike, and like Norris he was roundly booed. The crowd dispersed, exhilarated by the demonstration but dissatisfied with its result. Norris would be called on every day, shouted the leaders, until their demands were granted. The parade was an ominous portent of things to come.

The parade of May 31 had proved typical. The initiative in its organization had been taken by the returned soldiers who were in the lead, followed by civilians. The proportion between them was a matter of controversy: the *Western Labor News* assumed that the parade was all soldiers, while Captain Frederick G. Thompson, a returned soldier and barrister hostile to the strike, asserted that the proportion of soldiers was not very great.[5] Thompson admitted, however, that the first part consisted mostly of soldiers. Estimates of the size of the demonstration also varied, ranging between the ten thousand, reported by the *Western Labor News* and Thompson's figure of eight hundred.

Much to the alarm of Mayor Gray another parade had occurred on Monday, June 2. This time the marchers proceeded along Portage Avenue, enthusiastically booing Eaton's and the *Free Press*. Again they saw Norris and with the same result as on the previous Saturday.[6] On June 3 the parade had formed up, as on previous occasions, in the Market Square but repaired to near-by Victoria Park where Bray reported that a committee of soldiers had waited upon the premier with unsatisfactory results.[7]

Impatience among soldiers was not confined to the pro-strike element. Soldiers and others opposed to the strike soon began to organize counter-demonstrations. On Wednesday, June 4,

[4]Preliminary hearing, *The King* v. *William Ivens et al.*, testimony of Mayor Gray.
[5]*Ibid.*, testimony of Frederick G. Thompson.
[6]*Western Labor News*, June 3, 1919.
[7]*Ibid.*, June 4, 1919.

both sides staged parades. The two very nearly met in front of the legislative buildings as the anti-strike group had moved off just before the pro-strike group arrived. An onlooker watching one of the parades on Osborne Street was heard to enquire, "Which bunch is this?"[8]

At this point Mayor Gray, who had become increasingly alarmed at the possibility of trouble, had issued, on June 5, the first proclamation forbidding parades.[9] "In virtue of the authority vested in me," ran the solemn declaration, "I do hereby order that all persons do refrain from taking part in any parades." The proclamation had stopped the parades temporarily and on June 7 the Mayor had addressed a large meeting in Victoria Park. He was introduced by Bray and received quite a good hearing.[10]

However the parades had effectively shattered the strike committee's policy of inaction. Never again during the strike was order completely re-established. There were other indications of an approaching crisis. Tempers were becoming frayed by the long struggle, and on both sides there was a rising tension which boded ill. Public irritation was increased by a new and drastic step by the strike committee. On Tuesday, June 3, the committee, according to the *Western Labor News*, "decided to withdraw all workers who had been allowed to return to what we regard as vital industries."[11] The reason for this decision was obvious: having failed to secure their objectives through a policy of partial conciliation, the strike leaders now undertook to increase the pressure. It was hoped that intensification of the strike would force Premier Norris into the concession of collective bargaining. The strike could then have been terminated and declared to be a victory for labour. "If Norris says he will not budge," said the *News*, "then he must be made to budge." As a result the milkmen, breadmen and icemen again ceased work.[12] To meet this fresh emergency the companies

[8]*Ibid.*, June 5, 1919.
[9]Preliminary hearing, *The King* v. *William Ivens et al.*, testimony of Mayor Gray. *Western Labor News*, June 7, 1919.
[10]*Ibid.*, June 9, 1919.
[11]*Ibid.*, June 5, 1919.
[12]Preliminary hearing, *The King* v. *William Ivens et al.*, testimony of James M. Carruthers, Edward Parnell, and Charles H. McNaughton.

concerned had to make new arrangements. The Crescent Creamery, left with eight men, and some office staff, called in volunteers and carried on a partial service; milk was delivered in trucks to the various schools which had been established as distributing centres. The other milk companies adopted a similar policy. The bread companies, through the efforts of their officials and a few strike-breakers, continued to supply the retail merchants who collected bread at the bakery. The ice companies, like the creameries, delivered their product to the school depots.

The situation in Winnipeg had thus been rendered infinitely more acute after June 4. It was at this point that Canon F. G. Scott, the senior chaplain of the First Division in France, arrived in Winnipeg to make a gallant but unavailing effort at mediation. Never particularly interested in ideologies or political systems, he had an abiding interest in people. Hearing, in the East, that "his boys," the soldiers, were in trouble, he came to Winnipeg and tried to arrange a settlement between the contending factions.[13]

Unfortunately the strike had passed beyond the stage where efforts at mediation could even be seriously considered. It was about this time that the roof of the Children's Hospital was damaged by the severe storm of June 14. It was regarded as unsafe to relight the boilers and get up enough steam to keep the sterilizers and the laundry in operation. Yet, according to one member of the hospital staff, when two members of the metal workers' union appeared and offered to fix the roof, a member of the men's advisory council of the hospital said, in tones of "black hatred," to tell the men "that he would see them in hell first." Subsequently the volunteer workers repaired the damage but the incident revealed the state of irritation which now existed. In such an atmosphere Canon Scott could not possibly succeed in his endeavour.

While the strike continued in Winnipeg its repercussions widened throughout Canada. The *Western Labor News* of June 5 listed strikes at Vancouver, Calgary, Lethbridge, Edmonton, Saskatoon, Regina, Prince Albert, Brandon, Port Arthur, Fort William, Toronto, and a number of smaller places.

[13] *Western Labor News*, June 10, 1919.

Not all of these strikes were formidable and in some the situation had improved.   In Edmonton, where a general strike had been proclaimed on May 26, many had returned to work by June 10, although workmen in the railway shops and round-houses and some expressmen and teamsters were still out.[14]   A general strike had been proclaimed in Calgary but by June 4 conditions were beginning to return to normal.[15]   In Saskatoon where the general strike had reached serious proportions, the street-cars had begun to operate on June 9.[16]

In Toronto the general strike failed to reach the proportions which at one time had seemed likely.[17]   The turning point came in the small hours of Sunday morning, June 1, when the street railwaymen at a mass meeting in the Star Theatre decided not to take any part in the strike.   Two days later, on June 3, R. C. Brown, president of the Metal Trades Council, announced that the strike was over and asked those who had gone out in sympathy to return to work.

In other centres, however, strikes continued to develop. All the unions of Prince Rupert voted on June 9 for a general strike.[18]   On the same day the employees of the Moose Jaw Electric Street Railway Company struck for shorter hours and increased wages.[19]

Most ominous, from the viewpoint of those who feared a general western tie-up, was the Vancouver sympathetic strike.[20] Having been in the forefront of radical labour movements, the Vancouver Trades and Labor Council soon began to show concern for the Winnipeg strikers.   On May 22 the Council threatened to call a general strike vote if the military were used in Winnipeg.   Six days later the strike vote was ordered.   The motives of the Council were mixed, as its resolution indicated, but the immediate cause of the vote was the Winnipeg strike. The resolution listed seven demands which were to be "the

[14]*Daily Colonist,* Victoria, June 10, 1919.

[15]*Manitoba Free Press,* June 4, 1919.

[16]*Daily Colonist,* Victoria, June 10, 1919.

[17]*Mail and Empire,* Toronto, June 2 and 4, 1919.

[18]*Daily Colonist,* June 10, 1919.

[19]*Manitoba Free Press,* June 10, 1919.

[20]For material on the Vancouver strike I am very much indebted to Mr. Robert W. Prittie of the Department of External Affairs who sent me a number of excerpts from the *B.C. Federationist* of May-July, 1919.

policy of the workers in Canada now on strike, or about to come on strike in support of the Winnipeg workers." The first three, which referred directly to the Winnipeg strike, were: the re-instatement of the postal workers; the immediate settlement of their grievances; and the concession of the right of collective bargaining. That the Council was angling for support of the soldiers was indicated by demands four and five: pensions for soldiers and their dependents on the basis laid down by soldiers' organizations and a minimum gratuity of two thousand dollars for overseas service. Local grievances of a type general in the West were indicated in the last two demands: the nationalization of all cold storage plants, abattoirs, and elevators to prevent food hoarding, and the enactment of legislation to provide for the six-hour day in all industries in which there was unemployment. Failing the granting of these demands, threatened the Council, the workers would continue to strike until the resignation of the dominion government.

This programme was endorsed by a majority of the labour unions which voted upon it, though the majority was not nearly so overwhelming as in Winnipeg. The vote by unions was twenty-two in favour of the strike and fifteen against; by persons it was 3,305 in favour and 2,499 against. To a considerable extent the "yes" vote resulted from approval of the stated demands. In part, however, it was the product of other local grievances, particularly among the seamen, longshoremen, and shipyard workers. The size of the negative vote perhaps indicates the difficulty of effecting sympathetic action in centres remote from the scene of the original dispute, unless local grievances are sufficiently strong. Even though the vote was close the Council promulgated the general strike on the evening of June 2.[21]

On June 3 the Vancouver general strike began and nearly every branch of organized labour, with the exception of the public utilities, stopped work. Water-front activities were at a standstill and communications were partially paralyzed by the strike of street-car and telephone operators.[22] Also out were metal trades unions, meat cutters, brewers, loggers, sugar

[21]*Daily Colonist*, June 4, 1919.
[22]*Ibid.*, June 6, 1919.

refiners and several small unions. Estimates of the total number on strike vary from the 12,000 of the conservative *Daily Colonist* to the 60,000 of the pro-labour W. H. Crook.[23]

The strike assumed many of the characteristic features of its Winnipeg counterpart. Vancouver, like Winnipeg, had a strike committee which tried to avoid a collapse of society by keeping at work such essential employees as bakers, milk-waggon drivers, firemen, policemen, and hotel and restaurant employees.[24] The anti-strike elements organized the Citizens' Law and Order League which was supported by Premier John Oliver. Mr. Oliver declared his belief that the agitation was led by men who were determined to overthrow the constitutional government of the country. The Citizens' League organized a jitney service which largely neutralized the effects of the street-car strike, much to the anger of the Trades and Labor Council, and published a newspaper, the *Vancouver Citizen*.

The strike dragged on for a month but it never reached a crisis as in Winnipeg. Instead it gradually petered out and was formally ended by the Trades and Labor Council on July 3, a week after the collapse of the Winnipeg strike.[25] However, the electrical workers and telephone operators remained out until July 16.

Several reasons for the comparative placidity of the Vancouver strike may be suggested. It was the secondary phase of a dispute which had originated in Winnipeg and neither of the contending parties in Vancouver showed the same vigour or bitterness. The strike committee was more liberal in the number of services which were allowed to continue and the dominion government did not intervene. The fact that the Vancouver strike was shorter (four weeks compared with six) helps to explain the avoidance of disorder. The real crisis was reached at Winnipeg in the fifth week of the strike. There were no soldier parades in Vancouver. In a longer strike such parades might have taken place with their inevitable sequel of

---

[23]*Ibid.*, June 4, 1919; Crook, *The General Strike, Labor's Tragic Weapon*, 552.

[24]Also kept at work were laundry workers, ice-waggon drivers for delivery to hospitals only, ten members of the cemetery staff to dig graves, six caretakers in the water department and all theatre employees. Gas workers were to remain at work to furnish gas to hospitals and to firms producing foodstuffs.

[25]*Daily Colonist*, July 4, 1919.

government intervention and street disorders. Because the Vancouver strike was largely, though not entirely, a sympathetic strike, its end was foreshadowed by the collapse of the Winnipeg strike. It lasted for another week chiefly because the authorities had not been goaded into suppressive measures. With the strike in Winnipeg over, that in Vancouver lost an important source of encouragement, and local grievances were not strong enough to ensure its continuance, except by the electricians and the telephone operators.

One of the most active men in Winnipeg during the early days of June was Captain F. G. Thompson, a returned soldier who had just resumed his legal practice.[26] Captain Thompson became alarmed at the nature of the strike and set out to organize his soldier friends against it. First he urged the G.W.V.A. executive to abandon the policy of neutrality. Neutrality was all right at the beginning, he said, but the time for neutrality was past. Something must be done to counteract those elements which "were backing the sale of bolshevik literature." Thompson did more than plead with the G.W.V.A.; he set about organizing the anti-strike parades. "I went out," he said, "and knowing a lot of returned men, around town, I put my views to them—that something had to be done, and I got an auto and chased around to other places . . . and preached the word from mouth to mouth that we would have to parade as a counter to this other parade and set a time and place." In order to facilitate his activity Thompson formed a small executive which he named The Returned Soldiers' Loyalist Association. He was extremely impatient of any hesitation in dealing with the strikers and it seems likely that he helped to organize the special police who took over the defence of "law and order" on June 9.

There were many other indications of continued anti-strike activity. After the second walk-out on June 4 the citizens' committee showed increasing efficiency in the distribution of milk, bread, and ice.[27] The most important anti-strike measure

[26]Preliminary hearing, *The King* v. *William Ivens et al.*, testimony of Captain F. G. Thompson.
[27]*Manitoba Free Press*, June 11, 1919.

was the dismissal of the police force on June 9 and its replacement by special police.[28]   This was probably an inevitable step in the movement against the strike; it was regarded as necessary to secure a more dependable force if determined action was to be taken to deal with the strikers.   The Council was under heavy pressure to undertake stronger measures and Alderman J. K. Sparling, the chairman of the police commission, had conferred with representatives of the citizens' committee (Messrs. Godfrey, Ingram, and Sweatman).[29]

The police force had maintained good order in the city until about the end of May and the question was asked later whether it was wise to dismiss them.   However, the council had not felt much confidence in the police since the initial strike vote. The soldier parades had alarmed the city fathers, particularly after the invasion of the council chamber.   The police, it was felt, would at least have to be reinforced by specials.   Demands for increased protection were pouring in from breadmen, milkmen and others particularly after the second walk-out of June 4. The citizens' committee supported their demands.

Organization of the specials, under the command of a Major Lyall, was begun on June 5.   Many of the specials (estimates varied between 85 and 95 per cent) were returned soldiers.[30]   Some of them volunteered because of personal conviction and a sense of public duty; others were attracted by high pay and the prospect of excitement.

Once the specials had been organized the council was in a position to dismiss the regular police.   Meanwhile the police had been considering their reply to the council's ultimatum, presented at the end of May, that they sign pledges to abstain from sympathetic strikes.   When they indicated their refusal to sign the pledges unless given certain guarantees in writing, the council discharged all but fifteen of them.   At the same time the chief of police, Donald Macpherson, was replaced by the former deputy chief, C. H. Newton, who was assigned the task of reorganizing the force.[31]   The special police were then

[28]*Manitoba Free Press*, June 9 and 11, 1919.

[29]Preliminary hearing, *The King* v. *William Ivens et al.*, testimony of J. K. Sparling.

[30]See especially the testimony of Ray McDonald who was a special, *Manitoba Free Press*, March 1, 1920.

[31]*Manitoba Free Press*, June 12, 1919.

A MEETING IN VICTORIA PARK DURING THE STRIKE

SPECIAL POLICE MARCHING WEST ON PORTAGE AVENUE, JUNE 10, 1919

Winnipeg Trades and Labor Council

JAS. WINNING . . . . President
A. C. HAY . . . . Vice-President
J. L. McBRIDE . . . . Treasurer
E. ROBINSON, Secretary and Business Agent

OFFICE OF THE SECRETARY: LABOR TEMPLE
Phone Main 1721

Winnipeg, Man., _____ May 18th _____ 191_

To the Oil Companies Ltd.

Dear Sirs:-
        Your communications of the 19th inst, to hand has received attention by the Strike Committee. I am instructed to forward you the decision of Committee on the matter of Coal Oil and Gasoline
1st. That all farmers be supplied with the necessary Coal Oil to meet their requirements .

2nd. That Military , Police, Doctors, Health Officers, and Hospital Cars must be supplied with the necessary Gasoline for Professional Services

3rd. That Chauffeurs in the industries which have permission to operate, must have special permit from the Central Strike Committee

                    I am
                    Yours truly

                    Strike Committee.

A DIRECTIVE FROM THE STRIKE COMMITTEE TO THE OIL COMPANIES

PLACARD CARRIED BY THE MILK AND BREAD WAGGONS

SPECIAL POLICE RIDING WEST ON PORTAGE AVENUE, JUNE 10, 1919

SPECIAL POLICE IN FRONT OF THE CITY HALL, JUNE 21, 191

sworn in and vested with the maintenance of law and order in Winnipeg.

The appearance of the specials in the streets on June 10 was the occasion for the next serious incident, the so-called riot of that day.[32]   Two specials had been on point duty at the corner of Portage and Main.   The intersection was more built up at that time than later.   The Bank of Montreal, the C.P.R. ticket office and the firm of Osler, Hammond and Nanton occupied three of the corners, but on the north-east corner stood a whole section of small buildings which was later demolished.   Here stood the Bank of Ottawa, the Central Shop, and the C. V. Café. Above the Café was a famous Winnipeg landmark, the lighted billiard-player who nightly drove innumerable balls into their appointed pockets.   About 1 P.M., a large, hostile crowd collected around the specials and began to jeer at them and probably to shove them around.

Several abortive attempts were made to preserve the dignity of the law.   Mayor Gray drove to the scene of the disturbance and vainly expostulated with the crowd.   A detachment of special mounted police was dispatched from the direction of the City Hall and approached the intersection from Notre Dame Avenue.   It attempted unsuccessfully to disperse the crowd which rapidly increased in size until it extended down Main Street as far as Bannatyne.   Some of the specials were rather awkward horsemen and the crowd attempted to take advantage of their inexperience by frightening their horses and pulling them off.   Reinforcements of mounted specials rode up and temporarily dispersed the crowd which closed in again and retaliated with sticks and stones.

Several of the mounted specials were injured, including one who had a distinguished military career, Sergeant-Major Coppins, V.C.   Coppins reported that after reaching Main Street he was hit on the back by some missile.   Turning in his saddle he saw bottles and stones being thrown.   Finally he was hit by a large stone which broke two of his ribs.

Meanwhile the Mayor was having his troubles.   Shortly after 3 o'clock he returned to the City Hall and found, to his dismay, that a large parade was being formed in Victoria Park, presumably with the intention of moving on Portage and Main.

[32]Preliminary hearing, *The King* v. *William Ivens et al.*, testimony of Sergeant-Major F. G. Coppins, Mayor Gray, and Francis Edward Langdale.

Fortunately the Mayor located the leader of the parade (who it was he did not reveal at the strike trials) and urged him, under threat of force, not to parade up Main Street. After a conference among themselves, the organizers of the parade decided to adjourn.

Another effort was made to disperse the crowd at Portage and Main when, about 4 o'clock, some two hundred specials advanced on foot from the City Hall square. They were an orderly and determined-looking force and at first they appeared to have cleared the streets. However, the crowds closed in again and the disorders did not cease until the mounted specials were withdrawn at six o'clock.

The incident was the signal for violent mutual recriminations. The *Western Labor News* blamed the appointment of the specials upon the citizens' committee. The specials, declared the *News*, were many of them thugs who had spilled blood, "caused" booze to be sold openly on Main Street at fifty cents a drink, and allowed fifteen or twenty groups to carry on crap games for hours. Utter lawlessness had developed, said the *News* triumphantly, during the first twenty-four hours after dismissal of the regular police.[33] The *Free Press* published a stinging editorial, under the heading, "Fine Business This!", which began: "Young Winnipeg soldiers, recently returned from years of overseas service . . . were yesterday, on the Main Street of their home town, while engaged in the patriotic duty of protecting the peace, the victims of murderous assaults by riotous aliens."[34] The events of June 10 did much to worsen the strike situation. Tempers became still more frayed and both parties were more enraged and embittered. Further disorders were not far off.

Some efforts at negotiation were made early in June and they ended in an important announcement by the metal trades employers which probably had some influence on the subsequent course of the strike.

The actual negotiations between the strike leaders and others were not productive of an immediate result. Shortly

[33]*Western Labor News*, June 12, 1919.
[34]*Manitoba Free Press*, June 11, 1919.

after June 5 Canon Scott presided at a meeting at which the anti-strike soldiers including Captain F. G. Thompson met four members of the strike committee—Winning, Russell, Scoble, and Pritchard.[35] The discussion was not amicable and appears to have consisted in Thompson asking hostile questions and failing to receive satisfactory answers. He enquired, for instance, whether the strike committee endorsed the O.B.U. principle and, according to his own account, received a different answer from each of the four strike leaders.

A more direct effort to settle the original dispute in the metal trades was undertaken by H. E. Barker, chairman of the train service employees committee. Barker established communications with the Metal Trades Council and with the employers in the metal trades in an effort to secure agreement over the principle of collective bargaining. The negotiations showed some signs of promise at first but had finally collapsed by June 13.[36]

The secretary of the Metal Trades Council in a letter to Barker dated June 2 stated that the demands of the Council were:

1. That every man employed in the metal trades shops of Winnipeg and vicinity should have the right to belong to the organization covering his trade and should not be discriminated against for belonging to it.

2. That members of the various organized trades employed in the Metal Trades shops should have the right to present and negotiate schedules covering wages, hours, and working conditions, with the employers.

3. That after agreement had been reached and schedules signed, any grievance arising in any plant should be taken up by the shop committee.

The employers in the metal trades, in a letter forwarded by Barker to the Metal Trades Council on June 3, substantially accepted these conditions. There was, however, one important difference. The employers stipulated specifically that the metal shops "shall continue on an Open Shop Basis." This opening

[35]Preliminary hearing, *The King* v. *William Ivens et al.*, testimony of Captain F. G. Thompson.
[36]See correspondence published in the *Western Labor News*, June 20, 1919.

statement of relative positions was not followed by any further constructive discussion.

The metal trades employers, however, made a statement on June 16. Published in the Winnipeg papers, apparently without the strike leaders having been previously informed, it was apparently so conciliatory as to weaken the position of the strike leaders in the minds of at least some of their supporters.[37] The statement was signed by E. G. Barrett of the Vulcan Iron Works, H. B. Lyall of the Manitoba Bridge and Iron Works, and H. W. W. Warren of the Dominion Bridge Company. They submitted the following proposals:

1. That employees should not be discriminated against by employers or by other employees on account of membership or non-membership in any craft or organization.

2. The members of the various trade organizations employed in the three metal trade shops were to have the right to present and negotiate schedules covering wages, hours, and working conditions, to individual employers or collectively to the employers of the metal trades.

3. The employees who were members of the various metal trades organizations in the contract shops (not including the railway shops) were to have the right to elect representatives from among the employees of the firm or firms involved.

4. After agreements had been reached and schedules signed, grievances or differences were to be taken up as follows:
   (a) All complaints were to be first submitted to the superintendent in charge.
   (b) If he and the craft directly interested failed to reach a settlement, the matter should be taken up with the company by the committee representing the craft.
   (c) If a settlement still was not achieved the committee representing all the trade unions employed by the firm or firms concerned was to negotiate with the firm or firms.

5. If all these negotiations failed the duly accredited international officers of the metal trade organizations were to be called in to assist in effecting a settlement.

6. During the entire period of negotiations there was to be no lockout and no strike.

[37] *Manitoba Free Press*, June 16, 1919.

This statement by the metal-masters recognized one type of collective bargaining. However, it did not go so far as to recognize the Metal Trades Council as it had been organized in Winnipeg. The Metal Trades Council included not only metal workers in the three companies involved in the dispute, the so-called contract shops, but it also included representatives of other metal workers including those in the railway shops. Clause 3 of the offer of June 16 provided for a metal trades council which represented only the contract shops. The railway shops were specifically excluded. This would have meant that the new council would have been less representative and therefore less potent than the Metal Trades Council as it then was organized.

The proposal was also calculated to eliminate the possibility of the Metal Trades Council co-operating with all the other Winnipeg unions in a general strike. If the new metal trades council failed to achieve settlement of a dispute recourse was to be had, not to the Winnipeg Trades and Labor Council, but, by Clause 5, to the international officers of the unions concerned. It was the appeal of the Metal Trades Council to the Winnipeg Trades and Labor Council which had precipitated the general strike. The metal-masters no doubt argued that the international officers would be more reasonable than the Trades and Labor Council.

The offer, while it ignored the Metal Trades Council, went some distance in recognizing the position of unions and the right of collective bargaining. The result was to produce a change of heart in at least some of the strikers. A former member of the strike committee told the author that there was, as he put it, "a flattening out" of enthusiasm on the part of some of the strikers in the closing stages of the strike. The appearance of what looked to some like an olive branch stimulated the demand that the strike now be ended and a victory claimed. The C.P.R. carmen at a meeting of Jubilee Lodge No. 6 passed a unanimous resolution on June 17

that seeing that the principle of collective bargaining is now assured to the men engaged in the metal trades to an even fuller extent than is enjoyed by the men employed in the railroad industries, the object for which the strike was called, has been now won, we therefore urge that in the best interests of all concerned, the sympathetic strike should be called off, and the men allowed to resume work.[38]

[38]*Ibid.*, June 18, 1919.

On the same night the C.N.R. carmen of Northern Star Lodge No. 371 R.B.C. of A. passed a similar resolution.[39] These resolutions were detached examples, but they indicated, an attitude which was probably more widely held. So at least thought the *Free Press* which proclaimed on June 17, "Strike Showing Indications of Early Collapse."

While the city council and the provincial administration fumbled with the strike the dominion government and its representative in Winnipeg, A. J. Andrews, prepared for more drastic action. On the night of June 16-17 the blow fell and eight strike leaders were rounded up and imprisoned in Stony Mountain Penitentiary, Russell, Johns, Ivens, Pritchard, Queen, Heaps, Bray, and George Armstrong. In addition four less prominent strikers, who were unfortunate in having non-Anglo-Saxon names, Matthew Charitonoff, B. Devyatken, Oscar Schoppelrel, and Moses Almazoff, were arrested; Blumenberg, for whom a warrant was issued, escaped to the United States. The arrests were made in Winnipeg, except for Johns who was about to leave Montreal on a speaking tour in support of the O.B.U. and for Pritchard who was taken from a westbound C.P.R. train at Calgary and lodged in the Calgary city jail before his transfer to Winnipeg.[40] All were arrested upon information and complaint from a R.N.W.M.P. sergeant, A. E. Reames.[41] They were charged with conspiracy "to excite divers liege subjects of the King, to resist laws and resist persons, some being part of the police force in the city of Winnipeg . . . and to procure unlawful meetings, and to cause divers liege subjects of the King to believe that the laws of the dominion were unduly administered." They were also charged with the publication of "certain false and libellous statements" in the *Western Labor News.*

The arrests were the culminating step in a policy which had developed during the previous two weeks. Since the beginning, the government's attitude had been firm. This had been shown by the dismissal of the postmen and the mobilization of troops. Now a programme of drastic action was taken, largely through

[39] *Ibid.*
[40] *Western Labor News*, June 21, 1919.
[41] *Ibid.*, June 19, 1919.

the influence of the minister of justice, Hon. Arthur Meighen, that able and very determined man, of Ulster descent, who was resolved that the strike must be broken. Meighen showed his attitude in the full-dress debate in the House of Commons on June 2.[42] Urged by the Conservative member for North Winnipeg, Dr. M. R. Blake, to stamp out sedition, Meighen presented a closely reasoned analysis of the implications of the strike. "It is proved," he said, "by the example of Winnipeg, and indeed follows inevitably from the very logic of the situation, that a general strike to succeed or, indeed, to continue, must result in the usurpation of governmental authority on the part of those controlling the strike." He made it quite clear that the government proposed to end this usurpation.

To accomplish this purpose a most significant step was taken on June 6 when a bill providing for the deportation, under certain circumstances, of Canadian citizens was introduced in the House of Commons by Hon. J. A. Calder, a Saskatchewan Liberal who was minister of immigration.[43] There can be no doubt that it was the situation in Winnipeg which persuaded the government to introduce the amendment to the Immigration Act.[44] Section 41 of the Act had provided for the deportation of people other than Canadian citizens who had been convicted of one or more of a list of seditious offences. The amendment changed the words "any person other than a Canadian citizen" to "every person who by word or act in Canada seeks to overthrow," etc. Deportation proceedings would then be possible against Canadian citizens providing they had been born in some other country to which they could be deported. This amendment passed its three readings in the House of Commons in record time. "Very little discussion ensued," wrote Sir

[42]*House of Commons Debates*, 1919, pp. 3009-64.

[43]*Ibid.*, 2305, 3175, 3211-14. *Journals of the Senate, Canada*, 1919, pp. 224-5.

[44]The Act of June 6 was technically an amendment to a previous Act amending the Immigration Act. This previous amendment had passed the House on May 12 and the Senate on June 4 and was awaiting the royal assent when the second amending bill was introduced on June 6. This indicates that the second amending Act was hastily conceived, presumably in response to the strike. Otherwise the provisions would have been included in the first act of amendment. Both amending acts: "An Act to amend the Immigration Act," 9-10 Geo. V, c. 25, and "An Act to amend an Act of the Present Session entitled An Act to amend the Immigration Act," 9-10 Geo. V, c. 26, received the royal assent on June 6.

Robert Borden in his memoirs, "as the Bill was read first, second and third times and adopted with unanimity in about twenty minutes."[45]   On the same day, June 6, it passed the Senate and received the royal assent.

Strengthened in its position the government continued to be opposed to a policy of undue conciliation and instead prepared to arrest the strike leaders.[46]   On June 7, A. J. Andrews wired to Robertson in Ottawa giving him the details of an offer of the metal employers to settle the strike.   Meighen wired to Andrews on June 9 that a settlement on the terms proposed would be a triumph for the strike leaders.   On June 15, Robertson, who had returned to Winnipeg, wired to the Prime Minister that a clear-cut declaration of collective bargaining seemed to be justified and that one had been submitted to and accepted by the metal trades employers.   Presumably this was the offer which was published on June 16.   Robertson also said, in his telegram of June 15, that further action outlined in a telegram of June 13 was likely to be taken in twenty-four hours "which we anticipate will result in speedy and satisfactory conclusion of the trouble here."

Rumours of impending arrests circulated for several days in Winnipeg before the blow fell.   The *Western Labor News* on June 13 reported that between 100 and 150 strike leaders were slated for early arrest.   Just before the arrests Mayor Gray made a statement to the effect that there would be "something of importance to us all in twenty-four hours."[47]   This was taken by Gray's opponents to mean that he had previous knowledge of the *coup*, although this he later denied.   The editor of the *Free Press* had heard the rumours and warned the government in an editorial written before but published after the arrests, that the *Free Press* "emphatically dissociates itself from any Strong Arm policy of breaking the strike."[48]

The timing of the arrests was decided by A. J. Andrews who acted for the dominion government.   According to one of his

---

[45]*Robert Laird Borden: His Memoirs*, Toronto, 1938, II, 978.

[46]The exchange of telegrams between Ottawa and Winnipeg described in this paragraph was reported to the House of Commons by Hon. Peter Heenan in 1926 after he had secured access to the relevant files.   *House of Commons Debates*, 1926, pp. 4006-4007.

[47]Preliminary hearing, *The King* v. *William Ivens et al.*, testimony of Mayor Gray.

[48]*Manitoba Free Press*, June 17, 1919.

colleagues he hesitated to take the plunge and only yielded to the persuasions of his associates after a most protracted argument. Responsibility for the arrests, however, was shared by the dominion government which obviously supported the policy, although the initial pressure may have come from Winnipeg. Robertson's significant telegram of June 15 suggests that the decision had been made by June 13 after discussions in which he had participated and that his colleagues in Ottawa had been informed. Moreover the fact that the arrests were preceded by Mr. Calder's bill of June 6 suggests that both steps were part of a preconceived plan.

The arrests produced varied reactions. The *Western Labor News* denounced the action bitterly and reported that the soldiers who met in Victoria Park on June 17 cheered the imprisoned men and that the meeting was "electrified by the arrest" and "vibrant with emotion."[49] The *Winnipeg Evening Tribune* was non-committal and simply expressed the hope that the strike leaders would get a fair trial.[50]

The severest critic of the arrests was the *Manitoba Free Press*. A close associate of the editor, J. W. Dafoe, told the author how annoyed Dafoe was at the news. "The air was blue around the Free Press building." Dafoe felt that the strike was on the point of collapse anyway and that the arrests simply made unnecessary martyrs and bolstered the morale of the strikers. He said in an editorial of June 18: "Their arrests at this time may do the extremists an actual service. They were in the perilous position of leaders of a senseless criminal strike which was nearing the point of collapse. . . . Their arrest will enable them to pose as martyrs in the cause of the working-man and will also supply them with a plausible excuse for failure."

The government now had to consider how to deal with the arrested strike leaders. Meighen favoured speedy action and wired to Andrews on June 17, "I feel that rapid deportation is the best course now the arrests are made."[51] That the government were contemplating deportation proceedings was also indicated by Mr. Calder's wire of June 17 to the commandant

[49]*Western Labor News*, June 18, 1919.
[50]*Winnipeg Evening Tribune*, June 17, 1919.
[51]*House of Commons Debates*, 1926, p. 4007.

of the R.N.W.M.P. in Winnipeg: "You are hereby authorized under section 42 of the Immigration Act to take into custody and detain for examination for the purposes of deportation the several persons referred to in your telegram of the seventeenth."

Why the government abandoned the attempt to deport the strike leaders is not entirely clear. It is true that George Armstrong would have proved an embarrassment as he was born in Ontario and, therefore, could not be deported. All the others, however, had been born outside of Canada. It may have been felt that such drastic action as deportation would be unwise. Andrews wired to Meighen on June 21 that unless the arrested men had been let out on bail the strike committee would have instigated a riot. As it was, he added, the strike committee did all in its power to prevent the "red soldiers' parade" which started the disturbances of June 21.[52] Apart from the attitude of the strikers it may have been felt that deportation proceedings would receive an unfavourable reception in other parts of the country. A policy calculated to deprive Canadian citizens of a trial might have elicited some protest. The government acted wisely in abandoning its original policy.

In the small hours of Saturday morning, June 21, six of the strike leaders, Ivens, Russell, Queen, Heaps, Armstrong and Bray, were released on bail. Pritchard and Johns had not yet reached Winnipeg. The other four arrested men, all with non-Anglo-Saxon names, Charitonoff, Almazoff, Devyatken and Schoppelrel, were retained in custody.[53]

The *Western Labor News* of June 21 described the release of the six men in graphic language. E. A. Andrews, J.P., T. J. Murray, solicitor of the Trades and Labor Council, the twelve required bondsmen and a number of the strikers left the Labor Temple in motor cars at 1 A.M. and swung along Notre Dame Avenue towards the penitentiary. Arrived at Stony Mountain "in the dim twilight of early dawn" the twelve bondsmen and the officials were taken to the chief warden's office, leaving a group of forty or fifty strikers waiting outside the prison gates. Here they were joined by the six arrested men. Continued the *News*: "When they, already tinged with

[52]*Ibid.*
[53]*Western Labor News,* June 21, 1919.

the pallor of the prison, entered the room, there was a period of affectionate handshaking, then Magistrate Andrews read to each of the accused and his two bondsmen, the usual legal documents. By three [o'clock] they left the room and marched into the corridor." Outside the prison gates the released men were greeted by their waiting friends. Lunch was provided by the women for the six. Just as the dawn was reddening the east they began the ride home.

Less than twelve hours after release of the leaders the disorders occurred in front of the City Hall. The released men were not involved in the organization of the soldier parades nor in the resultant disturbances. The Robson Report was quite definite on this point and declared: "It should be said that the leaders who had brought about the General Strike were not responsible for the parades or riots which took place, and, in fact, tried to prevent them," Andrews's telegram about the "red soldiers' parade," quoted above, provides additional evidence. Nor did the leaders take any part in the direction of the strike during its last days.

The long-run consequences of the disturbances were profound and will be discussed below. The immediate result, as already suggested, was a number of casualties. There were two deaths: Mike Sokolowiski, who was killed instantly, and Steve Schezerbanowes, who was shot in both legs and died later of gangrene.[54] In addition, the hospitals reported thirty casualties, of varying degrees of seriousness, of which twenty-four were civilians and six R.N.W.M.P. officers. The police had suffered injuries from bricks or other missiles. Most of the civilians had been shot. How many people had been injured but not taken to hospital it is impossible to say. Undoubtedly many got home themselves or were rescued by friends.

The list of casualties throws some light on the vexed question of who composed the crowd on June 21. According to pro-strike opinion it was mainly returned soldiers and according to anti-strike opinion it was mainly enemy aliens. Neither view is completely correct. According to Mayor Gray, who was a

[54]*Winnipeg Evening Tribune*, June 23, 1919. *Daily Colonist*, Victoria, June 24, 1919.

hostile witness, the parade was organized by returned soldiers. Of the twenty-four listed civilian casualties only four, including the two who were killed had "foreign" names. However, there were probably many "aliens" in the parade. Captain Thompson's testimony in regard to the composition of a previous parade, even though he may have exaggerated the number of aliens, cannot be ignored. Probably the parade of June 21 was composed of much the same elements as those which preceded it. The preponderance of Anglo-Saxon names on the casualty list may in part be explained by the fact that injured aliens would be less likely to go to hospital. The parade was, therefore, a composite affair under the leadership of returned soldiers.

The riot produced violent denunciations on both sides. The *Western Labor News* on June 23 published a strong editorial entitled "Kaiserism in Canada" which subsequently landed the editor in jail. It read:

What shall the sacrifice profit Canada if she who has helped to destroy Kaiserism in Germany shall allow Kaiserism to be established at home? . . .

There may be those who think that the blood of innocent men upon our streets is preferable to a "silent Parade." There may be those who think their dignity must be upheld at any cost. But we fail to see the slightest justification for the murderous assault which was committed.

Anti-strike newspapers were similarly indignant on the other side.

Considerable controversy followed over the question whether the use of mounted police and troops on June 21 was justified. Whether or not the authorities were acting legally depends upon a second question: whether the silent parade was an unlawful assembly. The use of force to disperse an unlawful assembly was, of course, entirely legal.[55] What then constitutes an unlawful assembly? It was defined in Section 87 of the Canadian Criminal Code of 1919 as "an assembly of three or more persons who . . . assemble in such a manner or so conduct themselves when assembled as to cause persons in the neighbourhood of such assembly to fear, on reasonable grounds, that the persons

[55]See A. V. Dicey, *The Law of the Constitution*, London, 1902, p. 452.

so assembled will disturb the peace tumultuously, or will . . . provoke other persons to disturb the peace tumultuously."[56] The legal justification for the action of the authorities in Winnipeg depends, therefore, on the assumption that reasonable persons were afraid that the parade would lead to a breach of the peace. Opinions will, of course, differ on this point: according to one view the parade would have been only a peaceful protest; according to the other, it would have inevitably produced disturbances. The author is of the opinion that in view of the excitement prevailing in Winnipeg at the time and in view of the disturbances of June 10, the authorities had reasonable cause to fear a breach of the peace.

The disturbances and their suppression broke the back of the strike. As a precautionary measure Main Street was patrolled again on Monday, June 23, by soldiers armed with rifles and by the R.N.W.M.P. officers armed with carbines and revolvers, while trucks mounting machine guns drove slowly up and down. Hearing that another parade was to be organized at Victoria Park the authorities despatched specials who closed the park. Mayor Gray, who accompanied the specials, estimated that there were about four hundred present in the park at the time.[57]

The *Western Labor News* which had done so much to rally and guide the strike forces was formally banned by the authorities on June 24.[58] Until his arrest on June 17 William Ivens had been the editor. Afterwards J. S. Woodsworth, who had arrived in Winnipeg from British Columbia during the strike, assumed the editorship. He was assisted by Fred Dixon. After Ivens's arrest Woodsworth and Dixon went to the office of the *News* on Rupert Street and resolved to keep the paper going. Dixon said: "J.S., you act as editor and I'll act as reporter." So the paper continued to come out.[59] Woodsworth was arrested several days later, and Dixon carried on alone. It was Dixon who wrote "Kaiserism in Canada." Upon the formal banning of the paper, Dixon published the paper in

[56]Tremeear, *Annotated Criminal Code*, 1919, Canada, Sec. 87. Dicey's definition was similar, *The Law of the Constitution*, 450.

[57]*Winnipeg Evening Tribune*, June 23, 1919.

[58]*Manitoba Free Press*, June 24, 1919.

[59]Olive Ziegler, *Woodsworth, Social Pioneer*, Toronto, 1934, p. 98.

hiding as warrants were now out for his own arrest. When Ivens was ready to assume the editorship once more, Dixon walked into a police station and gave himself up.

The strike continued for a short time longer in an atmosphere of gathering doom. Most of the leaders, although on bail, had undertaken not to resume activity. Those who had not been arrested were afraid that the blow would fall. The authorities had intervened and were maintaining control of the streets with armed force. Reduced to a state of terror, the Trades and Labor Council capitulated and announced the end of the strike on Wednesday, June 25, six weeks less one day from the beginning of the strike.[60]

After an impressive display of united and disciplined action on the part of labour the strike had ended in ignominious failure. One may properly enquire why.

A weakness in the whole position of the strike committee resulted from failure to define its objective precisely. The general aims of the strikers were clear: they were demanding the right to a living wage and the right to collective bargaining. In the early stages of the strike it was also clear that in effect their demands meant recognition of the Metal Trades Council and the payment of higher wages in the metal industries. Since the dispute in the metal trades had precipitated the sympathetic strike, presumably a settlement of the initial conflict would have been followed by a general return to work. So much was reasonably clear until the end of May. In June the picture was complicated by demands of the soldiers that the provincial government should introduce legislation making collective bargaining compulsory. No one knew precisely what was meant by collective bargaining. Did it mean bargaining between a shop committee and the management of a single firm or was the bargaining agent of labour to be a more general body like the Metal Trades Council or the officers of a trade union? Even the labour group was not in complete agreement on the issue. When the metal trades employers on June 16 suggested a form of collective bargaining which would have side-tracked the Metal Trades Council, two at least of the striking unions, as shown above, were in favour of accepting the proposal.

[60]*Winnipeg Evening Tribune*, June 25, 1919. *Manitoba Free Press*, June 26, 1919.

Despite the ambiguity, the strike would have continued longer if it had not been for other factors. The citizens' committee decreased the effectiveness of the strike by organizing the various volunteer agencies. In conjunction with the press the committee mobilized opinion against the strike and convinced many people that it was an incipient revolution. Finally, the citizens' committee prodded the authorities into those decisive steps which finally broke the strike. The group which organized the soldier parades played into the hands of those opposed to the strike. The parades led directly to the dismissal of the regular police, to the use of specials, and to the disorders of June 10. The action of the dominion government and its local representatives was conclusive. The arrest of June 16-17 deprived the strikers of their ablest leaders and frightened those who were left. By this time the strikers were discouraged by the long-drawn-out struggle and by the fact that the strikes in other western cities were obviously petering out. The intervention of the R.N.W.M.P. and the military on June 21 and 23 completed the demoralization of the strike leaders. Convinced that the game was up they ended the strike.

Whether the arrests were a blunder, as Dafoe thought, or a sound stroke of policy remains to be discussed. Divisions had undoubtedly begun to appear in the ranks of the strikers by the middle of June and it was inconceivable that the strike could have continued much longer. On the other hand, a prominent member of the strike committee assured the author that, but for the intervention of the dominion government, the forces of labour would have been able to secure from the Norris Administration an act making collective bargaining compulsory. This could have been hailed as a great labour victory and the labour movement would have avoided the loss of prestige which it actually suffered. The "ifs" of history present a fascinating but treacherous field for speculation; one thing alone is certain, intervention by the dominion government smashed the strike but provided the western labour movement with a tradition of martyrdom.

There is room for disagreement over the expediency of certain specific actions by the government, yet it was almost inevitable that there should have been governmental intervention in Winnipeg. The reasons for this are inherent in the nature of a general strike. To such an extent does it shatter the texture of ordinary society that it must be followed by the assumption of political control on the part of the strikers or by the resumption of control on the part of the existing authorities. A labour critic of the strike described this dilemma with great cogency at the Trades and Labour Council on the twenty-fifth anniversary of the strike. He said that it is folly to attempt a general strike unless you are prepared to take over the state. The strike committee reluctantly assumed a few of the functions of government, i.e. in regard to food deliveries; but, with society apparently on the verge of collapse in Winnipeg, they made no further effort at the assumption of political control. Faced with this crisis the authorities, local and federal, were compelled by the logic of events to intervene.

CHAPTER FOUR

Strike or Revolution?

T o s o m e extent the legend of martyrdom which grew around the names of the strike leaders was a result of their sudden and dramatic arrest. To a greater extent it was the result of the bitter legal battle which dragged on for nearly a year and which ended in the conviction and imprisonment of seven of the accused men.

When the strike ended, the leaders, with the exception of Dixon, were out on bail. There was still doubt as to whether they would be deported or given a jury trial. The first objective of the accused was to secure a trial and to raise the money to finance an adequate defence. A Defence League was formed to publicize the issue and to raise money. The accused themselves gave considerable assistance to the League. During the period when they were on bail several toured various parts of Canada (Ivens went to Ontario) in order to raise the necessary funds. The *Western Labor News* gave vigorous support, seeking to dissuade the government from deportation proceedings under the amended Immigration Act. "Our forefathers suffered and fought for this right," declared the *News* on June 30. "It has always been regarded as the birthright of every Britisher, and as part of the long boasted British justice for all others."

To F. G. Tipping, a labour man of moderate views, who had not been seriously implicated in the strike, fell the task of going to Ottawa to intervene with the department of justice to secure a jury trial. Tipping's interview with Hon. Arthur Meighen was not without its element of humour. Tipping had addressed a trades union meeting the night before seeing Meighen. Parliament was at that time meeting in the museum as the parliament buildings had been burnt in 1916, and he had suggested facetiously that it would be appropriate if the government was embalmed and left in the museum. This indiscreet remark received headlines in an Ottawa paper. When Tipping was ushered in to see Meighen he was horrified to find the latter reading the report of his speech. The subsequent interview was stormy but the accused got their jury trial. The Crown elected to bring charges of seditious conspiracy against Ivens, Russell, Johns, Queen, Heaps, Pritchard, Armstrong, and Bray.

The indictment, certainly not a masterpiece of English prose, was long and redundant but can be summarized.[1]   The

[1]Summary of the Indictment, *The King* v. *William Ivens et al.*

1. That the accused conspired to bring into hatred and contempt the government, laws and constitution of the Dominion of Canada and of the province of Manitoba and to promote feelings of ill will between different classes of H. M.'s subjects and particularly between the workers and the employers.

2. That in the furtherance of this object they convened the Walker Theatre meeting of December 22, 1918, and the Majestic Theatre meeting of January 19, 1919, plotted an unlawful general strike, aided and abetted the holding of the Calgary convention in March, 1919, aided and abetted the publication of literature designed to facilitate the carrying out of their seditious intention, and assisted in calling the unlawful general strike in Winnipeg in May, 1919.

The strike was described as intended to paralyze all industry and business in the city; to endanger the laws, health, safety and property of the inhabitants; to challenge and usurp constituted authority; to set class against class and by fear and intimidation to compel large numbers of workmen to strike against their will.

The principal types of striking employees, many of whom had struck in violation of contracts, were listed. It was asserted that many had struck in violation of the Industrial Disputes Investigation Act of 1907 and Section 499A of the Criminal Code.

The strike committee, it was asserted, usurped the functions and powers of government in Winnipeg and dictated to the inhabitants the terms on which they could carry on business. The increasing demands and threats of the strikers, the parades and disorders of June 10 and 21 were described as further steps in the conspiracy.

3. That the intention of the accused was by means of the strike "to compel compliance with the demands of such workmen and employees who went out on said general sympathetic strike whatever such demands might be, and to bring about changes in the laws in force in said city of Winnipeg."

4. That the accused organized an unlawful combination of workmen and employees to compel compliance with the association's demand by means of unlawful general strikes which were intended to be a step in a revolution against the constituted form of government in Canada.

5. That the accused conspired to form an unlawful combination in order to obtain control of all industries in Canada and to obtain the property, both real and personal, rightfully belonging to other persons and combinations.

eight were accused of conspiracy to bring into hatred and contempt the governments of the Dominion of Canada and the Province of Manitoba and to introduce a Soviet system of government. The meetings at the Walker and Majestic Theatres, the Calgary convention, the publication of allegedly seditious literature, and the general strike were all described as means to achieve these objects. The strike was declared illegal and it was asserted that many of the strikers, who had broken contracts with their employers, had violated the Industrial Disputes Investigation Act of 1907 and Section 499A of the Criminal Code.[2]

The preliminary hearing occurred in the magistrates' court before Police Magistrate R. M. Noble in July and August and produced a number of sharp clashes. A. J. Andrews, K.C., and J. B. Coyne, K.C., appeared for the prosecution and E. J. McMurray, Hugh MacKenzie, T. J. Murray, and Marcus Hyman, for the defence. The great point at issue in the preliminary hearing as well as in the subsequent trials was whether evidence of the Crown, which was not connected directly with the accused, should be admitted. Crown witnesses dealt at length with the silent parade and the disturbances of June 21, which had occurred, according to the defence, in opposition to the wishes and efforts of the strike committee. The defence repeatedly objected on grounds of irrelevancy.

6. That the accused conspired to incite H. M.'s subjects in Canada to introduce in Canada by other than lawful means the "Soviet" form of government similar to that now in force in portions of Russia, by unlawful means, i.e. by unlawful general strikes of all workmen in Canada.

7. That the accused, by encouraging the general sympathetic strike in Winnipeg, after the strike had begun in the metal trades, conspired to commit a common nuisance as defined by Section 221 and 222 of the Criminal Code.

[2]Section 499 of the Canadian Criminal Code read in part as follows:

"Every one is guilty of an offence punishable on indictment or on summary conviction before two justices and liable on conviction to a penalty not exceeding one hundred dollars or to three months' imprisonment, with or without hard labour, who,—

(a) wilfully breaks any contract made by him knowing, or having reasonable cause to believe, that the probable consequences of his so doing, either alone or in combination with others, will be to endanger human life, or to cause serious bodily injury, or to expose valuable property, whether real or personal, to destruction or serious injury; . . . ."

See W. J. Tremeear, *Annotated Criminal Code, 1919, Canada*, Calgary, 1919, p. 633.

On this issue the court upheld the prosecution.   Said Magistrate Noble:

It having been shown that the accused were ringleaders during the strike which began on the fifteenth of May; having taken an active part throughout the strike, evidence of what others did, sympathisers or cooperators in that strike, what they said and did is admissible.   It is true they are not charged as conspirators here, but for the purpose of the admissibility of the evidence, I think their words and acts in connection with the strike are perfectly admissible.[3]

The issue came up again and again in the subsequent trials in the Court of King's Bench, and the attitude of the judge in the higher court was substantially the same as that of Magistrate Noble.

The difference of opinion on the admissibility of evidence arose from a difference of initial premises.   The prosecution assumed that the accused were ringleaders in a conspiracy.   If one accepts the assumption, the disputed evidence was no doubt admissible.   "Evidence is admissible of what was said or done in furtherance of the common design by a conspirator not charged, as against those who are charged, *after proof of existence of the common design*," wrote W. J. Tremeear, a standard authority on the Canadian Criminal Code.[4]   The defence refused to accept the premise either that a common design had already been proven or that it would be proven in the course of the trial, but in this they were not upheld by the bench.   The magistrate allowed the disputed evidence, presumably on the assumption that it was admissible since the common design had already been proven *by other evidence*.   In this decision he was in agreement with Tremeear's opinion cited above.   The defence did not accept the basic assumption.   The accused men were finally committed for trial.

When the eight strike leaders appeared in court at the end of November the Crown elected to try R. B. Russell separately. Trial of the other seven was held over until January.   Counsel for the prosecution in the Russell trial were A. J. Andrews, K.C., T. Sweatman, and Captain Sidney Goldstine.   W. R. Cassidy,

[3]Preliminary hearing, *The King* v. *William Ivens et al.*
[4]Tremeear, *Annotated Criminal Code*, 717.

K.C., of Vancouver, J. E. Bird, W. Lefeaux, and E. J. McMurray, appeared for the defence. Andrews led for the Crown and Cassidy for the defence.

Russell's trial was dramatic at times and produced many sharp clashes between counsel and also between defence counsel and the judge, Mr. Justice Metcalfe.[5] On one occasion when Cassidy tried to ignore one of his orders, the judge ordered the bailiff to remove him from court, but decided subsequently to let him off with a reprimand.

The basic issue in dispute between prosecution and defence was clear. The Crown claimed that Russell and the other accused had participated in a seditious conspiracy of which the Winnipeg strike was a part. The defence maintained that there had been no conspiracy, that the accused were not in political agreement and were in fact members of different political parties, and that the strike was what it purported to be, an attempt to secure the principle of collective bargaining. This basic dispute again produced sharp clashes over the admissibility of evidence and again the bench consistently upheld the Crown.

Mr. Cassidy insisted repeatedly that it was unfair to try the accused men together on a charge of conspiracy. The proper way, he claimed, would have been to try each man separately on a series of specific charges. "It is wholly to be reprobated," he thundered, "to throw a body of men together and try to convict A on what B or C said, and all that sort of rubbish. It should not be tolerated." Conspiracy, he reiterated, had not been proven. There was not one tittle of evidence showing connection between the eight accused persons or showing any common pursuit of the design charged in the indictment. "The accused," he declared, "have different labor affiliations: four of them are Socialists, four are not; and they have been shown by evidence to have been continually fighting among themselves."[6] Cassidy claimed that there was nothing sinister about

---

[5]The material on the trials of the strike leaders is derived chiefly from the files of the *Manitoba Free Press*, the *Winnipeg Evening Tribune*, and the *Western Labor News*, Nov.-Dec., 1919, Jan.-April, 1920.

[6]Armstrong, Russell, Johns, and Pritchard were members of the Socialist party of Canada. Queen and Heaps were Social Democrats.

Russell's actions, that they were attributable to the fact that he was a socialist (not an offence under the law) and a member of a trades union.

Andrews differed sharply with Cassidy and asserted that there was a common understanding among the accused which, from the evidence, the jury could not fail to see. The words of the conspirators were seditious, he said, because they were uttered under circumstances which made them likely to produce a breach of the peace. Thus the Walker Theatre meeting was seditious not only because of the resolutions passed "but because these resolutions were made the means of getting off inflammatory speeches." Running all through the labour literature of the period, he said, was an appeal calculated to rouse the passions. Russell, he asserted, was guilty of the offences charged if he had aided and abetted their commission. He then described at length the offences which Russell had allegedly aided and abetted such as breach of contract on the part of the employees which, in such cases as that of the firemen, endangered human life. Andrews closed with a bitter denunciation of the strike leaders. "Would you be prepared," he asked rhetorically, "to crawl to the Labor Temple and bow your head three times to the floor to get milk for the children of this city?"

Judge Metcalfe in his charge to the jury began by defining the law of sedition, quoting from the English legal authority, Archbold:

It embraced all those practices, whether by word, deed or writing, which fall short of high treason, but directly tend to have for their object to excite discontent or dissatisfaction; to excite ill-will between different classes of the King's subjects; to create public disturbances, or lead to civil war, to bring into hatred or contempt the Sovereign or the government, the laws or constitution of the realm . . . to incite people to unlawful associations, assemblies, insurrections, breaches of the peace.[7]

The judge repeatedly made the point already asserted by the Crown, that it was the circumstances under which words were uttered or deeds committed which tended to make them seditious. The definition, he said, did not prevent free discussion "unless

[7]*The King* v. *Robert B. Russell*, judge's charge, official report, Dec. 23, 1919, Prothonotary's Office, Manitoba Law Courts, Winnipeg.

the discussion takes place *under circumstances likely to incite tumult.*" "A torch applied to a green field," he asserted, "may not be likely to cause a fire, yet when the grass is ripe and dry a spark may cause a conflagration."

The judge was careful to point out that if the accused had spoken in good faith, without seditious intent, they were not guilty: "After all, Gentlemen, we do not send a man to the Penitentiary until the Jury is satisfied that there was guilt in his mind. . . . When a man is charged with a crime, the essence of the crime is the guilty mind; that is not peculiar to sedition."

In regard to conspiracy the evidence must show a common intention. "There must be a common design, otherwise it is not a conspiracy." He added, however: "The usual evidence in a conspiracy case is that the parties are shown to have pursued a line of conduct arising in the estimation of the jury from a common intention."

Judge Metcalfe then reviewed the various specific crimes which the accused were charged with conspiring to have committed. Most significant were his remarks on the general strike, which he described as illegal. "It is a serious offence," he said, "to conspire, combine or agree unlawfully to unduly limit facilities for transporting, supplying and storing commodities or to restrain trade." It was an offence for workmen to break a contract, knowing that the probable consequences would be to endanger human life, cause serious bodily injury and such. The judge asked:

How can a general sympathetic strike, the object of which is to tie up all industry, to make it so inconvenient for others that they will cause force to be brought about, to stop the delivery of food, to call off the bread, to call off the milk, to tie up the wheels of transportation—how can such a strike be carried on successfully without a breach of all these matters?

Judge Metcalfe's charge gives one the impression that he was trying to be fair but that he was convinced of the guilt of the accused. The jury brought in a verdict of guilty on every count. Russell, who was invited to speak before sentence was passed, suggested that he had merely acted as an official of a trades union and should not be regarded as individually responsible. "I carried out my instructions from the rank and file in the movement as a paid servant to the best of my ability," he protested, "and I feel that if the court had permitted me to demonstrate my real intentions during the strike I could have convinced everyone that it was free from anything criminal."

This line of argument did not move the court and Russell was sentenced to two years in the penitentiary. The defence appealed the case on a motion to quash the indictment and arrest the judgement. The appeal was, however, dismissed by the Manitoba Court of Appeal on January 19, 1920.[8] It was based upon questions of law involved in the judge's conduct of the trial, and its dismissal did not indicate an opinion by the higher court on the question of the guilt or innocence of the accused, but only on the question whether the trial had been properly conducted.

The trial of the other seven labour leaders, like Russell's, was chiefly a struggle over the issue whether the strike was part of a seditious conspiracy or a legitimate dispute over wages and collective bargaining. The second trial, like the first, was very long (January 22 - April 7) and was punctuated by sharp clashes between defence counsel and the bench. Four of the accused (Queen, Heaps, Pritchard, and Ivens) defended themselves in lengthy and eloquent speeches. The Crown was represented by A. J. Andrews, K.C., Isaac Pitblado, K.C., J. B. Coyne, W. A. T. Sweatman, and S. Goldstine. Counsel for the defence (i.e. for Bray, Johns and Armstrong) were respectively R. A. Bonnar, Ward Hollands, and E. J. McMurray.

The first week of the trial produced a fierce struggle over the composition of the court. The defence attempted to secure a postponement of the trial on account of the prevalent excitement which, they said, would make it difficult to secure an unbiased jury. Defence also moved for withdrawal of Andrews and Sweatman on the grounds that they had been actively connected with the citizens' committee and for retirement of the judge, Mr. Justice Metcalfe, from the case. These motions were all thrown out by the court.

The bitterest struggle occurred over the attempt by defence to throw out the entire petit jury panel. In making the motion

---

[8]Court of Appeal, *The King* v. *Robert B. Russell*, reserved case, Prothonotary's Office, Manitoba Law Courts, Winnipeg.

E. J. McMurray asserted that the Crown had been given a list of the jury panel before the trial, that the sheriff and deputy sheriff had not taken the names from the rolls in the proper order and that some fifty-eight names had been exempted from jury duty without affidavits being taken. The defence were suggesting that possible labour sympathizers had been omitted and that the names on the list of possible jurors had all been carefully investigated by the Crown before the trial.

To investigate these charges H. B. Webster, the foreman of the Grand Jury, and John G. Patterson, a county court judge, were appointed as triers. The key witness was the Deputy Sheriff, John Pyniger, who stated that the list of jurors had been given out to counsel both for the defence and the prosecution after receipt of an order from Mr. Justice Galt. He denied that anyone had been allowed to inspect the jury books. McMurray subsequently denied that he had heard of Mr. Justice Galt's order making the list of jurors available. John Queen produced an affidavit from a potential juror, Joseph Wright, who asserted that a mysterious visitor had questioned him about his attitude towards the trial. Mr. Justice Metcalfe however declared the affidavit useless as Wright was unable to identify his visitor. Defence motion to throw out the jury panel was rejected.

After the clash, the choice of a jury was a stormy process. On January 29 it was finally selected and sworn in. One hundred and ten jurymen had been called. Of these seventeen were peremptorily challenged by the defence. Forty-one were stood aside on grounds admitted by both defence and Crown. Seven were tried and found to be unfit to be on a jury; one was ruled unfit and stood aside at the request of the judge; thirty-one were stood aside by the Crown and one was peremptorily challenged by the Crown. The twelve jurors all came from rural Manitoba.[9]

The trial extended through February and March. The Crown called most of the witnesses who had already appeared in the Russell trial. Much of the trial was monotonous repe-

[9]The jury consisted of: D. Bruce, Carman district; George C. Glenny, St. Marks; A. H. Quick, Emerson; A. Davidson, Sperling; Herman Johnson, Lundar; J. M. Henderson, Hazel Ridge; George Morrison, Hazel Ridge; James Kirkpatrick, Ridgeville; John Stevens, Hazel Ridge; James Jack, Ridgeville; Thomas Spence, Greenridge; Alex Sinclair, Tyndall.

tition but there were occasional explosions.   Queen had a sharp exchange with Mayor Gray over their relations with each other on the food committee of the city council.   Bonnar denounced one of the Crown witnesses as a spy and suggested that he had been bribed to testify in the Russell trial.   A felicitous interlude occurred on February 21 when learned counsel congratulated the judge upon the occasion of his fiftieth birthday.   Afterwards hostilities were resumed.   The defence tried to make the point that the citizens' committee, rather than the strike committee, had stirred up class hatred and arrogated to itself the functions of government; but this line of argument was thrown out by the bench.   By the middle of March the evidence had been heard and the closing speeches began.

The final speeches of the four accused who defended themselves were herculean efforts.   All spoke at great length. Pritchard's speech when printed later was 216 pages in length. Heaps began with the intention of speaking for only two hours, concluding his speech about noon; but he was urged by Bonnar to extend it, and eventually spoke all afternoon.   The speeches of Queen and Ivens were also long.   All the defendants were beginning to show signs of strain in the closing phase of the trial.   Ivens was near collapse after addressing the jury for fourteen hours and even the urbane and genial Queen revealed his state of tension by nervous gestures and occasional difficulty in controlling his voice.

All the defence speakers hammered at the point that there had been no conspiracy.   There were touches of humour in Queen's speech; in one part he declared smilingly that the defence *claimed* that the Andrews, Pitblado, and Sweatman who were conducting the prosecution were the same Andrews, Pitblado, and Sweatman, who had worked on the citizens' committee.   In the main, however, his speech was deathly serious. He attacked the character of the Crown witnesses, many of whom he said were professional spies who earned their living by attending meetings and getting something on somebody.   He insisted that the strike itself was a legitimate effort to secure the principle of collective bargaining.   Especially he pointed out that the evidence had failed to connect him with many parts of the alleged conspiracy such as the Majestic Theatre meeting, the Calgary convention and the organization of the O.B.U.

Ivens claimed that the Crown had failed to establish the essential connection between all the alleged conspirators. He insisted that there were divisions in the labour party and quoted a newspaper reporter who had said that the two parties in the Labor Temple had fought like cats and dogs. "Some conspiracy," added Ivens drily.

Pritchard's speech was studded with witty sallies and literary allusions. The greater part of it consisted in the effort to show that both the socialist and trades union movements were legitimate and constitutional. They had been misunderstood, he said, by people who read into labour terminology alarming meanings which the words did not convey to labour men. "Revolution," he said was used much more casually by labour men and usually meant nothing more than change, not violence and bloodshed. Pritchard referred only briefly to his part in the strike. The evidence, he pointed out, showed that he came to Winnipeg some time after June 10 and left some time before June 17 and that he addressed a meeting of the Labor Church along with the Rev. A. E. Smith of Brandon and J. S. Woodsworth.

Ward Hollands, in defending Johns, argued that Johns was not present at the strike (he was absent in the East on a lecture tour in support of the O.B.U.) and that no evidence had been offered to prove that he had ever written a letter urging the workers of Winnipeg to strike.

The most successful of the defence speeches was made by Heaps. Without repudiating his colleagues or the labour movement he nevertheless contrived gradually to extricate himself from any connection with the alleged conspiracy. Bonnar who realized how well it was going down with the jury said to him, in the first interval, "Keep it up, son."

Most of this eloquence on the part of the defence was unavailing. Judge Metcalfe's summing up was much the same as in the Russell trial.[10] The jury found six of the seven guilty.

[10]The judge defined seditious conspiracy in terms similar to those he had used in the Russell trial. Again he made the point that the accused were guilty only if the prosecution could prove seditious intention. He repeated the point that utterances become seditious if made in circumstances when they are likely to create disorder. Again he covered the same ground: the Walker Theatre meeting, the Calgary convention, etc., pointing out those aspects of the evidence which the jury must consider.

Heaps alone was acquitted on all counts.   Bray, the returned
soldier, was convicted on the seventh count only and the other
five were convicted on all seven counts.

The verdict of the jury produced various reactions.   According to the *Free Press*,[11] the six men convicted accepted the verdict
quietly, but relatives and friends in the courtroom were deeply
affected.   When the first verdict of guilty was announced in
the case of Ivens, a groan escaped from the crowd, and as the
others were announced, the wives of several of the men broke
down one after another.

At first the crowd who thronged the corridors of the law
courts thought that the men had been acquitted and began to
cheer wildly.   The judge ordered the corridors to be cleared.
This was done by the police amidst the boos and jeers of the
crowd who had now learned the correct verdict.

A week later, on April 6, the convicted men were assembled
to have sentence pronounced.   While waiting for the court to
convene they conversed freely and apparently light-heartedly
with their families and friends.   John Queen in particular kept
the relatives of the prisoners laughing with his witty sallies.

Then came the sentence: a year in prison for each of the five
who had been convicted on all counts and six months for Bray.

More fortunate than Russell was Fred J. Dixon who was
tried in January and February, 1920, before Mr. Justice Galt
on a charge of seditious libel.   Dixon was in the historic tradition of Joseph Howe and William Lyon Mackenzie in electing
to defend himself.   Although not a lawyer he was well qualified
in many ways to undertake this task.   He was a fine-looking
man with a deep resonant voice which made a good impression
on the jury.   He had a remarkable grasp of English constitutional tradition and of the rights of the subject which it
allowed.   He was coached on the legal points involved by
L. St. George Stubbs with whom he spent a few days at Birtle.[12]
Dixon had an advantage over Russell and the others in being
charged with seditious libel, a more specific charge than seditious
conspiracy and easier to refute because it did not permit the

[11]*Manitoba Free Press*, March 29, 1920.

[12]Stubbs later had a stormy career first as judge and subsequently as member of
the provincial legislature.   His removal from the bench, as a result of the Macdonald
Will Case, was a *cause célèbre* in Winnipeg in the early thirties.

great body of evidence which the Crown used in the other cases. The charge was based on some of Dixon's speeches during the strike and particularly on two editorials, "Kaiserism in Canada" and "Bloody Saturday," which he had published in the *Western Labor News*.

Dixon conducted his defence with great skill and his final speech to the jury was a magnificent plea for the broad principles of British justice.[13] It was couched in simple, straightforward, and moving language. Dixon displayed a remarkable ability to consider the evidence, discard the irrelevant, and to hammer home the essential points. The real issue at stake, he insisted, was freedom of speech. "I want to emphasize the fact again that so far as liberty of opinion is concerned, that is what is on trial," he declared and continued: "Liberty of speech and the press have been secured by the fearless action of British juries and Canadian juries, and they can be preserved by the same method." He based his defence on the plea that his criticisms of government had been offered in good faith with the object of peaceful reform. "The issue," he said, "is what was my object in writing those articles? Was it to promote disaffection and bring about riots, or was it to secure a remedy by peaceful means?" His answer was that he had urged only peaceful reform. He denied having had a seditious intention. "I advised men to use their ballots and keep the peace. Surely that is not evidence of seditious intention when you advise a man to keep quiet." Dixon examined his articles in an effort to prove that they were written in good faith. Then in slow, measured tones he concluded with a moving appeal to the jury: "You are the last hope so far as the liberty of the subject is concerned. . . . In your hands is placed the question of liberty of speech. Whether a man has a right to criticize government officials or not." Despite a very hostile summing up from the bench Dixon was acquitted, after the jury had been out for forty hours![14]

Dixon's acquittal was followed by the dropping of similar charges against J. S. Woodsworth. Woodsworth had been indicted for publishing a number of specified editorials including

[13]*Dixon's Address to the Jury*, The Israelite Press Limited, Winnipeg.

[14]There is a tradition in Winnipeg that the jury were deadlocked for many hours owing to the refusal of one juror to vote for acquittal. Eventually, of course, he gave in.

Dixon's "Bloody Saturday" and "Kaiserism in Canada."[15] Better remembered is the fact that he was charged with the publication of two other "seditious libels," passages from Isaiah: x, 1 and LXV, 21-2, the latter of which read:

And they shall build houses, and inhabit them; and they shall plant vineyards, and eat the fruit of them. They shall not build, and another inhabit; they shall not plant and another eat; for as the days of a tree are the days of my people, and mine elect shall long enjoy the work of their hands.

On February 16, 1920, the day of Dixon's acquittal, the Crown entered a *nolle prosequi* on all counts against Woodsworth.

In addition to the trials of the strike leaders which attracted wide public attention, a number of other persons were prosecuted on such charges as unlawful assembly, disorder, riotous conduct, and interference. These cases all involved men who had been arrested on June 21. They were tried before a special court in which all were defended by T. J. Murray, solicitor for the Trades and Labor Council. The cases dragged on until December 1919. There were a number of acquittals, including Martin, one of the organizers of the silent parade of June 21. There were also a number of convictions. Sentences varied from five dollars and costs to two years' imprisonment, the latter given to a man named Krael who was convicted of rioting and unlawful assembly.[16]

[15]Court of King's Bench, Fall Assizes E.J.D. 1919, *The King* v. *J. S. Woodsworth,* Prothonotary's Office, Manitoba Law Courts.

[16]*Western Labor News,* June 30, July 9, 1919. *O.B.U.Bulletin,* Nov. 22, Dec. 6 and 13, 1919. The following convictions were reported:

Name	Charge	Sentence	Date of conviction
H. McKenzie	rioting on June 21	$ 20 and costs	June, 1919
K. Boal	"	$ 10 and costs	"
F. Donaldson	"	$ 5 and costs	"
George E. Jones	"	$300 or 30 days	July, 1919
Adolph Berrol	"	23 months	Nov. 11, 1919
Michael Krael	rioting and unlawful assembly	2 years	Nov. 27, 1919
—Sczaurski	unlawful assembly	1 year	Nov. 27, 1919
—Salsbury	intimidation	$25 and costs	Dec., 1919
—Easten	"	"	"
—Ruppel	"	"	"
—Wallbak	"	"	"
J. G. Flett	"	suspended sentence	"
A. Armstrong	"	"	"

None of the prisoners convicted before the court had played a part of any importance in the direction of the strike. In addition to those who were given the benefit of a trial a number of aliens arrested in connection with the strike were interned at Kapuskasing, Ontario, and some were probably deported.[17]

The convictions in the trials were all based upon the assumption that the Winnipeg strike was the result of a conspiracy to overthrow the government. Whether it was an incipient revolution is an issue which will be debated as long as the strike is remembered. Two juries were persuaded that a seditious conspiracy had in fact occurred. Yet, in a less hysterical atmosphere than existed in Winnipeg in 1919-20, there is still room to wonder whether they were right or wrong.

The question of the guilt or innocence of Russell, Johns, and their associates, is part of the more general question of what factor or combination of factors precipitated the strike. Certain long-run forces must be taken into account. The dispute preceding the strike did not come out of a blue sky. It came at the end of a series of controversies which had raged in a crescendo since at least 1917. A labour man who was not sympathetic to the strike told the author, "the situation was ripe for a strike—in fact it was over-ripe." There was a great deal of unrest in western Canada and the weapon of a general strike had been frequently discussed. Three times in 1918 the Winnipeg Trades and Labor Council had contemplated a general strike. Twice it had actually begun to take a strike vote. Both the convention of the British Columbia Federation of Labor and the Calgary convention had passed resolutions in favour of a general strike unless certain demands were secured. When the dispute developed in the metal trades in Winnipeg, the labour people immediately thought of a general strike because they had been talking about it for months.

The causes of the unrest were set forth in great detail in the reports of the two royal commissions which sat in 1919, one

[17]See *The Labour Gazette*, vol. 19, no. 10, Oct., 1919, pp. 1257-8; no. 12, Dec., 1919, p. 1468; *Canadian Parliament, Sessional Papers*, 1921, no. 18, report of the department of immigration for the year ending March 31, 1920; *Quebec Chronicle*, Oct. 28, 1919; *O.B.U. Bulletin*, Nov. 29, 1919.

under the chairmanship of Chief-Justice Mathers appointed by the dominion government and the other under H. A. Robson, K.C., later chief-justice, appointed by the Manitoba government.[18] Partly the unrest was the result of post-war reaction. "Minds had been intent on the War," said the Robson report, "and the efforts therefor and that engrossing fact having ceased, the relaxation caused concentration upon the real or supposed wrongs at home." There were many of these supposed wrongs. Unemployment was increasing in the West in the spring of 1919 and this made many labour men anxious to precipitate a showdown before it was too late. The post-war inflation was well under way. Everyone felt the high cost of living. Wages had not kept pace with prices. Winning, who testified before the Robson Commission, said that workmen were trying to maintain families on seventeen to twenty dollars a week. There was some real suffering in Winnipeg. A nurse who was in Winnipeg in 1919 wrote to the author: "All through the long drawn out strike of the metal workers union, the children of these men had been brought by their gaunt mothers to the hospital for treatment. The diseases they were suffering from were chiefly due to starvation and after they had been properly fed for a few weeks they were sent back to their poverty-stricken homes as 'cured'." According to both royal commissions the feeling of grievance was increased by the "ostentatious display of wealth" which the labour people encountered among other elements in Winnipeg. The housing problem was acute. Labouring people were exasperated by the scarcity of houses and by the poor quality of many which already existed. Finally, according to the Robson Commission, labour resented the refusal of many employers to accept collective bargaining.

In addition to these economic and social grievances, there were political grievances against restrictions upon freedom of speech, the prohibition of the importation of some radical literature, the slowness of the government to release political prisoners, and the dispatch of troops to Russia.

[18]*Report of the Royal Commission appointed under Order-in-Council (P.C. 670) to enquire into Industrial Relations in Canada together with a Minority Report* [The Mathers Report]. *Royal Commission to enquire into and report upon the causes and effects of the General Strike which recently existed in the City of Winnipeg for a period of six weeks, including the methods of calling and carrying on such strike.* Report of H. A. Robson, K.C., Commissioner.

Restless and aggrieved as they were, the Calgary convention and the steps taken to establish the O.B.U. had given many labour people renewed hope for the future. The argument so frequently put forward by labour people that the O.B.U. had nothing to do with the Winnipeg strike because it had not been formed is invalid. It is true that it had not yet been formally established, but it was in process of being so, and the views which had been put forward in urging its formation helped to produce a new militancy in the minds of western labour.

It is obvious that a critical situation had developed in Winnipeg and in the West generally by April 1919. Moreover, the special sense of grievance had been increased by the utterances of labour leaders, many of them socialists. "The general discontent among Labour," said the Robson Report, "has been fomented by the Socialist leaders." This leads to the great controversial question: did the small group of socialist leaders deliberately precipitate the strike in order to establish a soviet form of government? The question may be sub-divided into two parts: (1) Were the members of the socialist group (Russell, Johns, Pritchard, Armstrong, Ivens, Queen, Heaps, and Bray) likely to make a bid for political control at this time? (2) Were they in fact the decisive agents in precipitating the strike?

In attempting to answer the first part of the question it is necessary to consider the previous background of Russell, Johns, and their associates. It has already been shown in Chapter I that they represented an extension into Canada of European and especially British left-wing labour thought. Seven of the eight accused came originally from Great Britain. Armstrong alone was a native Canadian. Of the eight, the most influential and the men of ideas were Russell, Johns, and Pritchard. Russell and Johns were the moving spirits in the increase of radical influence in the Winnipeg Trades and Labour Council and in the establishment of the *Western Labour News*. They were joined by Pritchard in dominating the Calgary convention and in organizing the movement which culminated in the O.B.U. The others (Queen, Heaps, Ivens, Armstrong, and Bray) were valuable allies before and during the strike but were not so influential in the formulation of left-wing labour policy. Russell, Johns, Pritchard, and their significant literary ally,

J. Cooper, were in the tradition of British industrial unionism. A straight line could be drawn from Robert Owen and the Grand National Consolidated Trades Union, through the Social-Democratic Federation of the eighties and the syndicalism of James Connolly and Tom Mann in the early twentieth century to the group led by Russell and Johns.

The eventual objective of Russell and his associates was clear. They expected, once the O.B.U. was completely organized, to be able to dominate the country. The views were similar, on this point, to those of Owen, Hyndman, Mann, and James Connolly, who, for instance, had once said "Let us be clear as to the function of Industrial Unionism. That function is to build up an industrial republic inside the shell of the political state."

So much for the long-range objective, but one may ask where the Winnipeg strike fits into this grandiose scheme. Surely, if the country was to be taken over after the peaceful organization of the O.B.U., it was the wildest folly to jeopardize the whole scheme by a premature strike. It is of course possible that Russell and his associates intended to conduct a "general expropriatory strike" of the type proposed by French syndicalists as well as by the I.W.W. and by British industrial unionists such as Tom Mann.[19]

If this were the case one would have expected more evidence of preparation in the conduct of the strike. The record belies the idea that the strike was a premeditated attempt to overthrow the government. It is true that, just as in Seattle, the strike committee constituted a sort of *ad hoc* government which was probably illegal; but, as already shown, they were compelled to assume some functions of government simply to keep the wheels of life moving in Winnipeg. This assumption of control throws no light upon their attitudes towards the permanent problem of government.

The efficiency of the strike organization might perhaps be regarded as evidence of a premeditated conspiracy. Yet many of the acts of the various strike committees suggest improvisation rather than premeditated plan. The two strike com-

[19]Crook, *The General Strike, Labor's Tragic Weapon*, 213 ff. Webb, *The History of Trade Unionism*, 658.

mittees (the central strike committee and the general strike committee) were developed only after an interval during which the strike was directed by the *ad hoc* committee of five. The fumbling efforts of the strike committee to handle the problems of milk and bread deliveries and of the gasoline supply do not suggest that any previous thought had been devoted to these problems. Nor was there any direct evidence that the strikers really intended to take over the government. Presumably if the provincial government first and the dominion government later were to be overthrown force would have been required. Yet the strike committee never made the slightest effort to arm the strikers or to organize them in any way for fighting. The strategy of the strike committee was to keep the strikers off the streets and out of trouble. When disorders occurred they occurred contrary to the efforts and wishes of the strike committee. Keeping the strikers at home was scarcely the method to be used in staging an expropriatory strike or in setting up a soviet, but it was exactly the strategy which one would have expected in an orthodox strike over wages, hours, and the right of collective bargaining.

It might have been possible to argue that although the radicals did not plan the strike as a part of the conspiracy, yet they tried to use it as a means of revolution once it had begun. Even this assumption, however, will not square with the facts. The entirely peaceful policy of the strike committee and the absence of any attempt at force indicate that no effort was made to direct the strike into revolutionary channels, after it had begun.

It must always be remembered that even the extreme radicals like Russell were British socialists, not Russian revolutionaries. They might talk loosely about soviets; but there was nothing in their conduct of the strike to suggest the Russian tradition of terrorism and conspiracy. They were the forerunners of the I.L.P. and of the C.C.F. rather than of the modern Canadian communists who, to a much greater extent, are in the Russian revolutionary tradition.

Much more in accord with the evidence is the view that the radicals, perhaps carried away by the wave of emotion which swept the Winnipeg labour world, advocated the strike to secure a more limited objective. Radical syndicalists were quite capable of supporting limited strikes as a means to increase working-class consciousness and irritation against the capitalistic system.[20] Even if the radical leaders in Winnipeg were proof against the prevalent excitement, and this is doubtful, their followers were not. Russell claimed during the trial and has since maintained that he was opposed to the strike and only supported it in deference to the majority. Nobody believed him. Yet his claim may have been justified.

It seems obvious, therefore, that while the motives of the radicals were somewhat obscure, there was nothing in their conduct to indicate an attempt to overthrow the government.

The second part of the question, whether the members of the socialist group were the decisive agents in precipitating the strike, remains to be answered. Explanations which concentrate on the radicals tell only half the story. There can be no doubt that the decision of the Trades and Labour Council to stage a general strike was the result of a wave of feeling on the part of all elements in the Winnipeg labour world, radicals and conservatives alike. A significant indication of this was the personnel of the committee of five which directed the strike in its early stages. It was composed of three conservative trade unionists, Winning, Veitch, and McBride, one Social Democrat, John Queen, and one Socialist, R. B. Russell. Russell was not only the only socialist on the committee but the only member who had been associated with the formation of the O.B.U. Mr. Robson stressed the unanimity of labour opinion in support of the strike:

It is too much for me to say that the vast number of intelligent residents who went on strike were seditious or that they were either dull enough or weak enough to be led by seditionaries. The men referred to may have dangerously influenced certain minds, but the cause of the strike, and of the exercise of mass action, was the specific grievance above referred to [the refusal of collective bargaining] and the dissatisfied and unsettled condition of Labour at and long before the beginning of the strike.

In short, the strike was the result of a unanimous movement within the ranks of Winnipeg labour and was not instigated merely by a small radical group.

[20]Hiller, *The Strike*, 250-1.

One cannot escape the conviction that the real prisoner in the dock was the O.B.U. In a way the O.B.U. was a conspiracy to secure control of the country, just as had been the Grand National Consolidated Trades Union and the Social Democratic Federation. It seems doubtful whether Russell and his associates really contemplated the capture of political power.[21] Many radicals have talked about the dictatorship of the proletariat in much the same way that many professed Christians talk about the coming of the Kingdom of Heaven on earth. Whether or not the O.B.U. was a conspiracy, it was not a conspiracy against which legal action could be taken with any chance of success unless it could be connected with the Winnipeg strike.[22]

Many of the difficulties in the case for the prosecution arose from the effort to connect the O.B.U. with the strike. Of the accused, Russell, Johns, Pritchard, and Armstrong had been associated with the O.B.U.; but Pritchard and Johns had little to do with the strike. Pritchard was in Winnipeg only for a few days between June 10 and June 17 and Johns was away during the entire six weeks. To be sure they may have been more remotely connected with the strike, but they did not actively promote it. This is particularly surprising in the case of Johns who enjoyed a position of leadership in the Winnipeg Trades and Labor Council. If the strike were part of a premeditated conspiracy one would have expected him to share its direction with Russell. Others of the accused, Queen, Heaps, Bray, and Ivens, were active in the strike but did not participate in the organization of the O.B.U. A third group, the orthodox trade unionists such as Winning, Veitch and McBride, was very influential in precipitating and directing the strike, but had serious political differences not only with the O.B.U. group but with Queen, Heaps, Bray, and Ivens as well.

[21]The O.B.U. preamble was much milder than that of the I.W.W. While looking forward to the day when production for profit would be replaced by production for use, the O.B.U. preamble urged nothing more drastic than education of the workers "in preparation for the social change" and the formation of a workers' organization. Its object was to enable the workers "to more successfully carry on the everyday fight over wages, hours of work, etc., and prepare themselves for the day when production for profit shall be replaced by production for use." See Savage, *Industrial Unionism in America*, 185-6, 200.

[22]Legal action was not of course taken against the O.B.U. as such but against its leaders.

This means that if the O.B.U. and the strike are to be connected the link must be Russell and Armstrong. Armstrong, "the soap-box orator of considerable ability," while no doubt influential, was not of first-rate importance. This line of reasoning would place tremendous importance on Russell, the only man of first-rate ability who was associated with both the O.B.U. and the strike. His motives in supporting the strike were open to several interpretations and, even if one assumes that he hoped to precipitate a revolution, it appears unlikely that all his associates were dupes.

It is therefore the opinion of the author that there was no seditious conspiracy and that the strike was what it purported to be, an effort to secure the principle of collective bargaining.

CHAPTER FIVE

Reconstruction

In the spring of 1921 Ivens, Johns, Queen, Armstrong, and Pritchard were released. Russell and Bray were already free.[1] All entered a world which had changed since the strike. Reconstruction had run its course in Winnipeg, and it was a generation which knew not Joseph. The temper of Winnipeg labour had changed. The collapse of the strike and the difficulties of readjustment had told. Gone was the exuberant recklessness of 1918-19. There was no abandonment of the struggle for reform, but counsels of moderation now secured a better hearing and men were disposed to accept gradual, step-by-step progress. No longer did anyone anticipate sudden Utopia. Already the old leaders were being forgotten. They must reassert themselves or forfeit their positions of importance.

After the strike it had remained to gather up the threads and to resume normal life in Winnipeg. Some of the damage could not be easily repaired. A residuum of hatred remained and is still in evidence after the lapse of a quarter of a century. The normal workings of the city's economy were gradually restored. The strikers who still had jobs returned to work. Some were not permitted to return. Postal employees and telephone workers who had ignored the order to resume work were permanently displaced. Reinstatement was refused to 403 postal employees, 119 telephone workers, and 53 firemen.

[1]Bray had completed his six-months sentence. Owing to the efforts of the Trades and Labor Congress which pressed the authorities for clemency, Russell forwarded a personal appeal and was released on parole on Dec. 11, 1920.

Many leaders in the strike movement were not re-employed, particularly in the civic services such as the police force and the fire brigade. There was evidence that the same thing happened in the railway services and quite likely elsewhere.[2]

Changing conditions made the re-employment question more difficult. Business in general had been seriously disrupted and both Winnipeg and its rural hinterland felt the effects. Much business had been diverted from Winnipeg, although it is impossible to estimate the amount. The farming community had felt the loss in having the Winnipeg market closed during the most active part of the season. The Canadian Northern Express Company usually handled daily 400 cans of cream and 1200 dozen eggs. For a time this business was completely cut off. The effect of the strike on the housing situation was unfortunate. The Robson Commission reported that at least 150 houses which had been commenced in the spring and which could have been completed by the autumn had been abandoned. Winnipeg did not immediately recover from this disruption; the level of prosperity was not so high after the strike as before it and many businesses required fewer employees. Many strikers were not reemployed because places were being made for returned soldiers who continued to be a first charge on business in the period of post-war reconversion.

Many strikers were ill-prepared to encounter this difficult period because of losses already suffered. At least 20,000 had lost their entire revenue for six weeks and many more were out for a part of the period. Particularly serious was the loss to employees in the building trades which could operate only for seven months of the year. They were out from May 1 to the end of June. To a lesser extent the professional classes suffered, since many abandoned their ordinary activities to help maintain community life. The city was put to great expense, a load which fell, of course, on the taxpayers. The cost of the special police force alone was $210,000.

Less easy to remedy than economic dislocation was the residuum of hatred. Few people who had any connection with

[2]*Royal Commission ... upon the causes and effects of the General Strike ... in the City of Winnipeg*, H. A. Robson, K.C., Commissioner, 1919; *Western Labor News*, July 2, 1919.

the strike can speak of it without emotion. Among a few neutral observers the strike produced a greater awareness of labour's position in the community and of labour's problems. "I still cling stubbornly to the belief," wrote the superintendent of nurses of a Winnipeg hospital, "that the Winnipeg general strike served a useful purpose. It made the people of Winnipeg realize that no modern community can function without the workers who carry on the humble and monotonous tasks which make a city safe and healthy to live in. It drew attention to social and economic abuses which have since been remedied, at least in part." Almost equally sympathetic to labour was H. A. Robson, K.C., chairman of the royal commission which investigated the causes and conduct of the strike. Mr. Robson condemned the leaders but showed great sympathy for the sufferings of the workers. "It is more likely," he said, "that the cause of the strike is to be found under the other heads [other than unemployment], namely, the high cost of living, inadequate wages . . . , profiteering." Great inequalities of wealth existed in Canada, he said, and "Winnipeg unfortunately presents a prominent example of these extremes." The capitalist system should continue, said Mr. Robson, but he added:

It is the affair of Government to see that these two important factors maintain proper regard for each other. If Capital does not provide enough to assure Labour a contented existence with a full enjoyment of the opportunities of the time for human improvement, then the Government might find it necessary [to step] in and let the state do these things at the expense of Capital.

He added that adequate medical service, adequate facilities of higher education, the latter practically closed as they were to the children of the workers, should be made available to labour. To lower the prices on consumer goods in Canada he suggested that a system of co-operatives be developed. He strongly recommended that the Industrial Conditions Act of Manitoba, providing for a joint council of industry to investigate and arbitrate disputes, should be brought into operation at once.

There were perhaps not many in Winnipeg outside the ranks of organized labour who entirely approved of Robson's recommendations; but they suggest that the strike may have been more effective than was apparent in 1919 in calling public attention to the plight of some of the workers.

On the other hand was a widely held resentment against labour and a strong conviction that the Criminal Code must be strengthened to provide against events similar to those in Winnipeg in 1919. Largely as a result of the strike, the Canadian Criminal Code was amended in July 1919 by the passage of Section 98.[3] It defined "unlawful associations" as those which propose or defend the use of violence to bring about either political or economic change. It provided that the property of such an association could be confiscated on suspicion and without warrant. The penalties for membership in such an organization ranged up to twenty years. The section stated further that any person who attended a meeting of such an association could be presumed to be a member of it. The issue of proof to the contrary was upon the accused. Importing or distributing the literature of such an association also carried with it a maximum sentence of twenty years. At the same time, parliament repealed Section 133 which guaranteed the right of free speech by explicitly stating that no one should be deemed to have a seditious purpose who intended in good faith to point out the mistakes of the government.

Section 98 remained an object of criticism and attack by liberals of varying political affiliations until its final repeal at the instigation of M. Lapointe, the minister of justice, in 1936.

Despite the long aftermath of mutual resentment the strike instilled a greater moderation into capital and labour alike. Having gone through a protracted period of upset, each hesitated to goad the other to a point where a similar struggle might occur. It can hardly be denied that the strike greatly hastened the readiness of Canadians to accept modifications of a laissez-faire policy. These would have come anyway, but they might have been greatly delayed and have been achieved with great rancour, had it not been for the impression made by the strike on the Canadian—especially the western Canadian—mind. The chief result of the strike was that it had no sequel.

After the strike, the organization of the O.B.U. continued in Winnipeg and in the West generally. Whether the strikes

[3] 9-10 Geo. V, c. 46.

retarded or advanced the movement is a matter of question. Several of the leading members, particularly Russell and Johns, were occupied in the movement for their own defence during the last half of 1919 and were in prison in 1920 so that the movement was denied the use of their services. On the other hand, the strike had produced an impressive example of labor unity. The strikers in Winnipeg had developed an organization which had functioned in a most disciplined and efficient manner. Although the strike had ended in disaster it may well have encouraged the people who had been involved in it to renewed efforts.

At any rate the progress of the movement in 1919 was rapid.[4] In Vancouver, which had given a strong lead to radicalism, the Trades and Labor Council became identified with the O.B.U. early in July, severing its connection with the Trades and Labor Congress of Canada and with the A.F. of L. After this, the metalliferous miners of British Columbia, previously affiliated with the International Union of Mine, Mill and Smelter Workers, held a meeting in Nelson and formed a mining department under the name District No. 1 of the Metalliferous Miners of the O.B.U. The organized coal miners of Alberta and of eastern British Columbia who had been members of District 18 of the United Mine Workers of America abandoned the international body and became part of the new movement. At Prince Rupert the unions of fish packers, teamsters, metal trades and lumber workers, as well as the Trades and Labor Council, likewise joined.

In Edmonton also the movement made progress. Branches of the Carpenters, United Mine Workers, and the International Association of Machinists joined it, although this action involved expulsion from the local trades council.

In Winnipeg, despite the crushing defeat of the strike only three weeks before, a vote taken by the Trades and Labor Council went in favour of the O.B.U. by 8,841 to 705. As a result the Council adopted the O.B.U. constitution and requested all unions affiliated with the Trades and Labor Congress and with the internationals to withdraw and affiliate with the new organization.

[4]Logan, *The History of Trade Union Organization in Canada*, 397-408. *Tenth Annual Report on Labor Organization in Canada,* for the calendar year, 1920, Department of Labour, 1921.

Only in the conservative East did the movement fail to gain appreciably. J. B. Knight toured Ontario and Quebec but met with limited success. He remarked somewhat acidly, on his return, that the East was backward in labour mentality.

While the O.B.U. appeared to be carrying all before it, the conservative reaction set in and gathered weight. Three men, R. A. Rigg, William Varley, and Alfred Farmilo, the latter for many years secretary of the Edmonton Trades and Labor Council, were despatched to attempt to recapture the ground lost by the internationals in western Canada. Meanwhile the internationals had been busy circularizing their local branches. Some individuals who had remained silent at the Calgary convention now came out in open opposition to the O.B.U.

In the campaign strong support was secured from many employers who discovered hitherto unsuspected virtues in the international trades union movement. District No. 18 of the United Mine Workers of America, located in Alberta, was an example. Here the miners had deserted the U.M.W.A. and on December 1, 1919, they formed District No. 1, Mining Department, O.B.U. The U.M.W.A. head office accordingly revoked the charter but dispatched a commission to clear up the confusion. The commission was able to bring back some branches into the U.M.W.A. in August 1919. During the negotiations between the miners and owners in 1919 the latter demanded as a condition to reinstatement of the strikers that officers representing the miners must be vouched for by the international executive and some assurance given that the terms of agreements negotiated would be fulfilled.

Even in cities where the Trades and Labor Council had seceded, representatives of the Trades and Labor Congress were sometimes able to maintain a nucleus affiliated with the Congress. In Winnipeg Rigg, on behalf of the Congress, called a special meeting at which a press committee was appointed to regain control of the *Western Labor News*. As the president and secretary of the old Trades and Labor Council refused to surrender the material property in the press organ, the O.B.U. was deprived of both the press and the property.

The O.B.U. formed the Winnipeg Labor Council on August 5, 1919, with W. H. C. Logan, president, R. Bray, vice-president, and R. B. Russell, secretary-treasurer. Publication of the *O.B.U. Bulletin*, a vigorous exponent of the movement's philosophy, was begun in Winnipeg at the same time.

In Vancouver, the O.B.U. was successful in getting control of the property and funds of the Trades and Labor Council as well as control of the *B.C. Federationist*. However, Farmilo, acting on the instructions of the A.F. of L., secured the old charter of the council and set up a new council. In Prince Rupert two competing Trades and Labor Councils functioned in the latter part of 1919.

By the end of 1919 the movement had probably reached its peak and reported a membership of 41,150, organized into 101 local units with eight central labour councils and two district boards. The coal miners had seventeen branches in British Columbia and Alberta while the metal miners had ten local units. The movement was also strongly represented among the railway, lumber, and general workers.

In 1920 it made further gains but also sustained some important reverses. The metal mining district of northern Ontario went over to it after the collapse of a strike which had been weakly supported by the miners' and smelters' international. In addition further gains were made among the coal miners of Vancouver Island.

On the other hand a controversy which developed at the Port Arthur convention of the O.B.U. led to the secession of the lumbermen, a serious loss. The dispute arose over the question of organization. According to the O.B.U. system, all the units in a geographic area were linked and there was to be no connection between the various units in the same industry. This principle the lumbermen refused to accept and they refused also to abolish their central headquarters. At the Port Arthur convention only seven out of the ten delegates of the lumbermen were seated and, as a result, all but one withdrew. Later the Lumber Workers' Industrial Union took a referendum vote and severed its connection with the movement.

Conservative opposition to the O.B.U. was redoubled. The struggle was particularly acute in the Alberta and British Columbia mine-fields. Here the operators continued to oppose the O.B.U. and gave substantial wage increases to members of the U.M.W.A.

The conservatives were assisted by an important legal decision brought down in Winnipeg by Judge Prendergast on October 28 in a dispute between local lodge No. 6 of the Brotherhood of Railway Carmen and the carmen's O.B.U. council. The carmen's council had possessed itself of $847.85 which had been paid as dues to Lodge No. 6 before disruption. Judge Prendergast found that property of local unions which had been acquired by them as members of international bodies belonged to the members who remained loyal to the parent organization.

The release of Russell, Pritchard, and Johns brought some strength to the O.B.U., but its later history nevertheless was one of gradually declining influence. The released leaders toured the West in 1921 but reported that under existing conditions of unemployment (the post-war recession was under way) further organization was hopeless. By the end of 1921 a number of prominent leaders including Johns, Knight, Midgley, and P. M. Christophers (Christophers had the unpleasant experience of being kidnapped while working the Saskatchewan minefields in 1920)[5] had resigned from the union. The membership of the organization, according to the general secretary, had shrunk to about 15,000.

The centre of the movement was then and still is in Winnipeg, where headquarters had been moved in September 1920 after Vancouver had failed to pay its dues. There the street-railway operators and some general workers stood firm, but the great promise which the movement seemed to hold out in 1919 had obviously faded by the end of 1921. Actually there were large elements of the labour group, particularly skilled workers such as electricians, photo engravers, and so forth, who had never been touched by the O.B.U. at all. The list of affiliates in Winnipeg, where the movement made greatest progress, indicates that support came largely from comparatively unskilled workers. The list is as follows:[6]

[5]Christophers, former president of District Lodge 18 of the U.M.W.A. and latterly a member of the executive board of the O.B.U. had gone into the coal districts of Saskatchewan in July 1920 to organize branches of the O.B.U. He was kidnapped on July 4 and deported to Noonan, N.D. Five men were arrested. On October 12 at Estevan a judge dismissed charges against two and, subsequently a jury found the other three not guilty. Christophers resigned as an officer of the O.B.U. on October 23, 1920.

[6]*Tenth Annual Report on Labor Organization in Canada*, 1920.

Winnipeg Central Labor Council
Bakery and Confectionery Workers' Unit
Barbers' Unit
Building Trades' Unit
C.P.R. Unit
Fort Rouge Railway Workers' Union
General Workers' Unit
Ladies Garment Workers' Unit No. 1
Metal Trades' Unit
Railroad Unit No. 1
O.B.U. Railroad District
Running Trades' Unit (railroad employees)
Steam Shovel and Ditchmen's Unit
Steam and Operating Engineers' Unit No. 1
Street Railway Employees' Unit
Tailors' Unit No. 11
Teamsters' Unit
Women's Labor League.

Eventually most of these affiliates forsook the O.B.U. and the great experiment had failed.

It may be asked why the O.B.U., after early successes, declined into insignificance. An obvious reason was the unpopularity of the effort to organize all members by regions rather than by industries. This rejection of a basic attitude in the minds of many labour men lost the movement the support of the lumbermen, a disaster from which it did not recover. No doubt also, insistence on the regional principle prevented many potential members from ever joining. The I.W.W., which was based on the idea of industrial unions joined at the top, did not make this mistake.

A more fundamental reason for O.B.U. failure was that the craft union movement in Canada was already comparatively mature. The O.B.U. made little headway against it in the East and was unable to prevail against it permanently in the West. There was always a strong suggestion of the exotic about the movement and its organizers, who were plumped down, complete with Marxist jargon, in a Winnipeg in which craft unionism was already strongly established. A more authentic Canadian strain was represented by J. S. Woodsworth who was critical of attempts to explain the Canadian situation in terms of Old World philosophies.[7] The O.B.U. was the product of British industrial unionism. Owing to the ability of its advocates, and to unsettled conditions, it had a considerable impact upon labour thinking and flourished briefly. However, it was out of sympathy with the more conservative trade union tradition of Canada and was unable, in the long run, to stand against it.

Of greater long-run importance than the O.B.U. was the continuance of labour political activity in Manitoba. The O.B.U. was based on the idea of non-intervention in politics, but this principle was rejected by the Winnipeg group which founded the I.L.P. in 1920, a Social Democratic party.

Labour political activity in the West was, of course, not as important as the great indigenous agrarian movement which swept two farmer provincial parties into power and enabled the federal Progressive party to secure sixty-six seats in the election of 1921.[8] Yet, as one of the movements leading to the founding of the C.C.F., it was of considerable significance. The I.L.P. was organized in December 1920 by a group of which the chief members were Dixon, Woodsworth, and S. J. Farmer.[9]

The immediate reason for its establishment was a quarrel in the Winnipeg board of of the Dominion Labor party between Dixon and Farmer on the one side and right-wing labour elements which had been critical of the strike. This had led to the resignation of Dixon and Farmer from the Dominion Labor

[7]J. S. Woodsworth, "Business Man's Psychology," *Western Labor News*. Woodsworth objected to the rigid application of Marxist concepts to Canadian conditions. To call Canadian businessmen "bourgeois" he regarded as unsound. "We have," he said, "no class corresponding to the bourgeoisie class in Europe. Our 'middle class' occupies a very different position from what in Europe is known as the 'middle classes.' Most of our wealthy men have not inherited their wealth and by no means live an idle, self-indulgent life." "Those who have come to Canada in recent years, especially to Western Canada," added Woodsworth, "often fail to understand the Canadian life of a generation ago in which the men past middle age were nurtured." Woodsworth argued that the average Canadian businessman, having spent his early years on a farm or in a small town, had become isolated from any contact with the common people after moving to the city. He failed to understand the problems of the common man, not through perversity, but merely because he had no contact with them. Very often, said Woodsworth, the businessman was the victim of the "system."

[8]Wood, *Farmers' Parties in Canada*. Morton, *The Progressive Party in Canada*.

[9]Farmer had a long career in Manitoba labour politics and was leader of the C.C.F. group in the provincial legislature.

party which had been formed in 1918.[10] The I.L.P. was provincial in scope and had branches in Brandon, The Pas, Souris, and Dauphin, as well as Winnipeg. It drew support from three provincial sources: socialists like Heaps, trade unionists, and Methodists. The influence of Methodism in the rise of the I.L.P. was a factor of considerable importance. Humanitarianism has frequently carried Methodists into political radicalism;[11] Woodsworth and Ivens, both ex-Methodist ministers, were examples of this phenomenon.

The I.L.P. was the heir to several older parties since it drew support from the Socialist party of Canada, the Social Democratic party and the Dominion Labor party, none of which continued after 1920. Many former supporters of the O.B.U., including Johns, abandoned the view that it was useless for labour to participate in politics, and supported the new party. It was a middle-of-the-road party and included all varieties of labour politics except the two extremes, i.e. the right which still supported the older political parties and the left which pushed off into communism and formed the Workers' party.

The I.L.P. advocated an extensive programme of social amelioration in the early twenties. Woodsworth, who was elected as member for Winnipeg North Centre in 1921, asserted

[10]The Dominion Labor party which functioned in Winnipeg in the period 1918-20 was formed after the passage of a resolution of the Trades and Labor Congress of Canada in 1917 recommending the organization of a national labour party for Canada. Inaugural meetings were held in Winnipeg on Oct. 31, 1917, and at the end of Jan. 1918. On March 8, 1918, *The Voice* announced that the Dominion Labor party, i.e. the Manitoba section of the national Canadian labour party, had been created and that its constitution had been passed and was in effect. It was violently opposed by Russell, Armstrong, and others of the Socialist party of Canada. On July 15, 1920, Dixon was elected chairman of the Winnipeg branch of the party. The quarrel, which hastened its dissolution, occurred over the slate of candidates in the Winnipeg civic elections of 1920. Dixon and Farmer, the vice-chairman and the mayoralty candidate respectively, protested against the candidature of W. H. Hoop for Alderman. Dixon alleged that Hoop in a debate in Winnipeg in Aug. 1920 had described the strike as an attempt to smash the state and to set up a Russian Soviet government. Hoop denied having said this and insisted on running despite demands for his withdrawal. Farmer and Hoop were both defeated. See *The Voice*, Oct. 19, Nov. 2, 1917, Feb. 1, March 8 and 22, 1918; Logan, *The History of Trade Union Organization in Canada*, 283-284.

[11]A. R. M. Lower, "Two Ways of Life: the Primary Antithesis of Canadian History," *Annual Report of the Canadian Historical Association*, 1943. See, however, S. D. Clark, "The Religious Sect in Canadian Politics," *American Journal of Sociology*, November, 1945.

in his maiden speech in the House of Commons: (1) that it was the responsibility of the state to provide suitable work for the 200,000 unemployed in Canada; (2) that unemployment schemes were a first charge on the credit and resources of the country; (3) that the system of government-owned railways should be "further extended"; (4) that the national debt should be reduced by a "levy on wealth"; (5) that the state should assume the control of Canada's resources which was maintained by private individuals and corporations, particularly the banks and other financial institutions; and (6) that the state should "bring together these great factors, labour, natural resources and the equipment which we already have in such abundance in Canada."[12] In the budget debate, Woodsworth demanded "certain minimum standards involving proper conditions of livelihood for every man and woman and child in the country." Most characteristic of the socialist and humanitarian attitude of the I.L.P. was his plea:

I submit that the Government exists to provide for the needs of the people, and when it comes to a choice between profits and property rights on the one hand and human welfare on the other, there should be no hesitation whatever in saying that we are going to place the human welfare consideration first, and let property rights and financial interests fare as best they may.

The I.L.P. derived considerable impetus from the Winnipeg strike. The long struggle had given to labour a sense of solidarity and of effectiveness, and the prosecution of the strike leaders, as J. W. Dafoe had predicted, created a martyrology. Woodsworth, who remained the member for Winnipeg North Centre from 1921 until his death in 1941, was regarded as a hero who had been in prison. Heaps who joined him in the House of Commons in 1925 as the member for Winnipeg North and who held the seat until 1940, had been tried, but acquitted in 1920. To a great extent the early popularity of both was the result of their records during the strike.

Even more indicative of the influence of the strike was the performance of the Manitoba Labor party, which was merged with the I.L.P., in the provincial election of 1920. The most significant feature of the election was the display of strength of

[12]*House of Commons Debates*, 1922, pp. 84-91, 2248-50.

the United Farmers of Manitoba which elected 8 members (in a legislature of 55) although the provincial executive had not campaigned and had not drafted a platform, but of considerable significance also were the gains of the Manitoba Labor party which elected eleven of the seventeen candidates which it ran. Indicative of the influence of the strike trials was the fact that Ivens, Queen, and Armstrong, who were in prison, were elected by large majorities, while Fred Dixon held the seat which he had secured in 1914. "You will have noted the results of the Manitoba Election," wrote Dafoe to a friend. "The outstanding feature, of course, was the strength displayed by labor. They will have nearly 25% of the membership of the next legislature and, with perhaps one exception, all the labor members elected are reds."

In civic politics also labour strengthened its position as a result of the strike. In the Winnipeg elections on November 20, 1920, the Dominion Labor party soon to be replaced by the I.L.P., elected three aldermen and three school trustees.

Between the two movements of protest in the West, farmer and labour, there was little contact. The reasons have already been suggested. Such co-operation as there was in the Progressive movement between farmers and urban labour was verbal, or merely local, and determined by the character of certain constituencies. The Non-Partisan League in Alberta which was largely responsible for forcing the U.F.A. into politics, had some urban supporters including William Irvine, a young Scottish minister who published the *Alberta Non-Partisan* in Calgary, and J. S. Woodsworth who canvassed for the league in Southern Alberta in 1918.[13] After the disbanding of the Non-Partisan League, Henry Wise Wood succeeded in excluding from the political organization all who were not members of the U.F.A. This forced out Irvine and his associates who had unsuccessfully opposed the policy of exclusion. The Manitoba Labor party made some effort at capturing rural support in 1920 by including in its platform one or two planks, such as direct legislation through initiative, referendum, and recall, which were calculated to attract rural votes.[14] The results of the

[13]Morton, *The Progressive Party in Canada.*
[14]*Tenth Annual Report on Labor Organization in Canada,* 1920.

election must have been disappointing to anyone who expected much co-operation between farmers and labour. Of the eleven labour members, four were from Winnipeg and four were from the environs of the city (Assiniboine, Kildonan-St. Andrews, St. Clements, and Springfield). Of the remaining three, Dauphin was a railroad town, Brandon an urban centre, and St. George a small constituency composed mainly of Icelandic fishermen who elected a member named Kristjanson. None of the purely rural constituencies elected a labour member. Dixon, who had been a single-taxer, made some effort to hold farmers and labour together. But the single-tax was never very popular with the farmers and after Dixon's retirement from politics in 1923 even the link of his personality was removed.

The reasons for the failure of farmers and labour to co-operate in the West are clear. Yet they had much in common; both the labour and agrarian movements were phases of the revolt of western regionalism against eastern dominance. The farmers had as their immediate objectives the reduction of tariff duties and freight rates which, in their opinion, had been kept high by selfish eastern interests. The objectives of western labour radicals grew out of resentment against the conservatism and supposedly outmoded policies of eastern labour. When the reaction of the East to the strike became clear, particularly after the passage of section 98, western labour began to feel that the real enemy was the eastern capitalist. After 1921 this impression appeared to be confirmed by eastern opposition in the House of Commons to the policies of J. S. Woodsworth. Eventually farmer and labour developed the same bogey-man, eastern business interests.

Yet no political party in the twenties made any real attempt to unite labour and the farmers in a united party of protest. It remained for the C.C.F. to attempt this feat in the years after 1933.

It was ironic and significant that the real heir to the Winnipeg strike was J. S. Woodsworth, who had played a comparatively minor part. Heaps also derived prestige from the strike but he was always second to Woodsworth. There were several reasons for Woodsworth's assumption of leadership. Since he had not been subjected to the mental strain of a long trial and subsequent imprisonment, he emerged from the strike comparatively unscathed. Such was not the case with the more prominent strike leaders. All had gone through a trial by fire and none emerged completely unchanged. They were tired, emotionally and spiritually. They lacked their earlier resiliency. Their wives too had suffered. Two of these women were co-workers in the labour cause and continued eager for the fray. The others were more interested in home and children. They regarded imprisonment as a disgrace and, when it was over, they were anxious that their husbands should not occupy positions of dangerous prominence.

Most of the leaders continued with active and honourable careers in the labour movement; but none was so dominant as before. Partly this was a result of loss of prestige after collapse of the strike; but the men themselves had not the same drive. To some extent also, concentration upon specific tasks helped to divert their attention from the advocacy of a general Utopia.

Johns, for instance, was essentially a teacher. Before the strike he had enjoyed instructing his fellows in the principles of industrial unionism. Afterwards he fought a courageous battle to re-establish himself. Returning to his studies, he passed his matriculation and was appointed a machinist teacher in St. John's High School. His old-time drive and enthusiasm as a teacher was now diverted into instruction in purely mechanical subjects, but he felt the same satisfaction which he had formerly derived from the advocacy of industrial unionism. Later he secured the degree of Master of Education and was appointed Director of Technical Education for the Province of Manitoba.

Several of the leaders later sat in the provincial legislature: Armstrong from 1920 to 1922, Ivens from 1920 to 1936, and Queen from 1920 to 1941. Yet even with these men, concentration upon specific issues diverted attention from active leadership in a movement of general reform.

Most unchanged was Queen who had a distinguished career in municipal politics: he was seven times mayor of Winnipeg. Russell had a long career as secretary of the O.B.U., a position which he still occupied in 1948. Ivens, who had probably suffered the most, was particularly effective in the legislature and later became an able organizer for the C.C.F. Pritchard had a long career in municipal politics in British Columbia.

He was for some years reeve of Burnaby and was also chairman of the Union of B.C. Municipalities and of the Unemployment Committee of the Union of Canadian Municipalities. He was active in launching the C.C.F. in British Columbia.

Of the less prominent leaders, Bray became an O.B.U. organizer. Later he settled down in North Vancouver and concentrated on the raising of gladioli. Blumenberg emigrated to the United States where he worked with labour and socialist elements in Minneapolis and later in Duluth. He worked as a labour organizer in the iron ore area near Duluth and ran for municipal office on the socialist ticket.

These were all honourable records; yet none of the strike leaders assumed the position of leadership in the political labour movement which was achieved by J. S. Woodsworth in the years after 1919. Woodsworth inherited the martyrology of the strike. He was popularly supposed to have been the principal leader in it. Actually he had arrived in Winnipeg late in the strike and had taken no part in its direction although he had made speeches and had edited the *Strike Bulletin* for a few days after Ivens's arrest. He had been in prison for only a few days before the charges against him were dropped. Almost forgotten after 1919 was the important part played by Russell, Johns, Armstrong, and the other leaders.

This should not be taken as implying any discredit to Woodsworth who pursued a peculiarly disinterested and gallant career in support of what he considered the interests of the common man. It should merely be noted that Woodsworth's association with the strike gave him certain advantages in the effort to secure popular support. On the other hand, not having been too deeply involved in it, he was less hated by the business-men than some of the others. The author was told by a Winnipeg colleague that "Businessmen who fought the strike hard, within fifteen years were making a great deal (in private) of Woodsworth." There were other reasons for this cordiality. Woodsworth's policy was more moderate and gradualist than that of the syndicalists and industrial unionists of 1919. Through Woodsworth some of the influence of western discontent was carried into national politics without the extreme radicalism of some western labour leaders.

Index